Praise for *Soul S[ensing:]*
[Staying in Touch] With Yo[ur Loved Ones]

"FINALLY! A medium book that does what it says it's going to do, written by an author who truly cares about you and your deceased loved ones. Janice Carlson is the 'real deal.' I've known Janice for more than 20 years and she still amazes me with what she is able to bring through when talking to my loved ones who have passed over—both two legged and four legged. *Soul Sensing* is a book you will turn to again and again. I highly recommend it to all."

—Linda Abel,
The Medieval Chronicle

"This book, though a thorough and comprehensive reference book on how to communicate with our loved ones who've passed, is more than that. It is about teaching us to use capacities that have lain dormant because our culture doesn't nurture the qualities of intuition, right-brain development, listening and sensing messages from life and the dead—among a host of other psychic skills. Janice nurtures us through exercises and fostering awareness of the possibility to develop these. The precious outcome offers us a much more spacious and expansive view of ourselves and the universe. This is a meticulously written book covering all the bases for learning to hear and speak to those in the afterlife. Highly recommended."

—Lynn S. LaFroth,
Essential Wellness E-magazine, www.esswellness.com

"A gentle and loving guide to staying in contact with departed loved ones, both people and pets. Janice Carlson draws on her extensive experience as a medium to show how the dead reassure us with signs of their presence, and how we can communicate with them. *Soul Sensing* will help you validate your experiences and develop your own natural ability to reach out to the Other Side."

—Rosemary Ellen Guiley,
co-author, *Talking to the Dead* (Bestselling author, featured on The History, A&E, and Discovery channels.)

"Remarkable! *Soul Sensing* is enormously validating. The author described experiences that I have had and struggled to dismiss. My cat curling up beside me in bed for months after he passed. The hair on top of my head stirring in still air. The smell of my uncle's cigarettes in a non-smoking house. I could list the items forever. She makes sense of it all. She also encourages the reader to trust his or her own perceptions and develop the 'soul senses' that we all possess to some degree. This book combines a unique description of reality with practical how-to techniques on a subject that fascinates and challenges."

—Jinjer Stanton,
Author of *Yoga for Every Room in Your House*

Praise for Janice Carlson's afterlife-communication abilities:

"Janice's accuracy was astonishing. She's one of the best mediums I've ever encountered and I can't recommend her highly enough."

—Trish MacGregor,
International astrologer & Author of *Sydney Omarr Presents*

"Janice Carlson was so accurate. She zeroed in on family issues that I never even knew existed. When she accessed her accurate information from my deceased parents, it all made sense. She's uncanny. Her reading helped me immensely. Highly recommended."

—Phyllis Galde,
International Publisher, *FATE* magazine

"Janice Carlson is a medium with a message! And that message is from the Other Side in an up-close and personal way. My sister Dee and I experienced a medium session with Janice that we found captivating. Janice seems to have agility walking between worlds."

—Lynn LaFroth,
National Publisher, *Essential Wellness* newspaper

"Janice is connected! Her ability to communicate with our lost loved ones is truly a gift."
—Bobbi Smith,
New York Times **Bestselling Author**

"I first met Janice Carlson as a screenwriter, but she has morphed into a legitimate medium. I was very impressed, and I can assure you I am not easily impressed."
—Patrick Wells,
Internationally known **Movie Producer** of such films as
Young Blood and *I Love You To Death*
(starring William Hurt & Kevin Kline)

"For years, no one could give me a reading that was accurate, so I started to believe that it was no longer possible. Then I asked for a session with Janice. Her connection to the Other Side was instantaneous. She brought through confirming information that no one outside my family could know, and then went on to provide insights that I am still using every day."
—Michelle Lamb,
New York Times-featured Trend Expert & co-owner of Marketing Directions, Inc.

"Janice possesses a fantastic ability to reunite us with loved ones from the Other Side. She brings their message through loud and clear … and with love."
—Rob MacGregor,
Author of *PSYCHIC POWER: Discover and Develop Your Sixth Sense at Any Age*

"Janice has been instrumental in helping me adjust to my husband Peter's passing. Her role as a medium has been multifaceted and evolving, beginning with the first session when she first helped give a voice to Peter."
—Laura Kroeten Bue,
Clinical Psychologist
(widowed in 2005 and a regular client of Janice Carlson)

"This medium can give you all the answers you request. I had questions about family, friends, and pets who are on the Other Side. Janice answered all of them."
—Millie Gemondo,
Co-author of *Animal Totems* and
Animal Intuitive for 45 years

"Janice Carlson's ability to pick up on information about loved ones who have passed on is fascinating. She accurately described some attributes of my parents, a couple of friends who have gone on, as well as my beloved dog. Having had numerous psychic readings over the years, this was my first time with a medium whose focus was on giving me information from those close to me who have died. It was inspiring!"
—Nancy H. McMoneagle,
(**Internationally known** astrologer, writer, and **Director of Operations** of Intuitive Intelligence Applications, which she co-owns with her husband of **remote-viewing fame, Joseph W. McMoneagle**)

"I found Janice to be warm, open, friendly, and amazingly compassionate. Her skills in working with others show a tremendous capacity to empathize with her clients and to understand their heart deeply. She lovingly guided me through a session and I was amazed at the relevance and the insight she offered. It does not matter what one believes in, she is able to explain what she does in ways that are respectful to one's own spiritual outlook. She is, in short, a gifted healer and I am grateful that she is on the MyLovingTribute.com site."
—Eric Meyer,
Certified Grief Counselor & Licensed Traumatologist

"It was an incredible experience to speak with Janice. She has an amazing gift."
—Viv Ortiz,
Psychiatric Emergency Nurse

Soul Sensing

How to Communicate With Your Dead Loved Ones

by

Medium & Psychic

Janice Carlson

Authors' Direct Books—Founded in 1998
Chanhassen, Minnesota

© Copyright 2013 Janice Carlson.

Printed and bound in the United States of America. All rights reserved. No part of this book may be reproduced or transmitted in any form or by any means, electronic or mechanical, including photocopying, recording, or by an information storage and retrieval system, with the exception of reviewer who may quote brief passages in a review to be printed in a newspaper or magazine without written permission from the publisher. For information, contact Authors' Direct Books at P.O. Box 665, Chanhassen, Minnesota 55317.

This book includes information from many sources and gathered from hundreds of medium sessions by the author. Although all of the accounts in this book are true, the names and some specifics of the author's clients and their relatives have been changed in many cases in order to preserve their anonymity. This book is sold with the understanding that neither the author nor the publisher is engaged in rendering psychological, spiritual, legal, accounting, or other professional advice. The publisher and author disclaim any personal liability, directly or indirectly, for advice or information presented within. Although the author and publisher have prepared this manuscript with great care and diligence and we have made every effort to ensure the accuracy and completeness of the information contained within, we assume no responsibility for errors, omissions, inconsistencies, or carelessness with or misuse of the exercises and practices suggested herein.

ISBN: 978-0-9665887-1-2

Publisher's Cataloging-in-Publication
(Provided by Quality Books, Inc.)

    Carlson, Janice.
      Soul sensing : how to communicate with your dead loved ones / by Janice Carlson.
      p. cm.
      Includes bibliographical references and index.
      LCCN 2013930611
      ISBN 978-0-9665887-1-2

      1. Spiritualism.   I. Title.

BF1261.2.C37 2013   133.9
                         QBI13-600013

This book is available at quantity discounts for bulk purchases. For information, contact Authors' Direct Books at P.O. Box 665, Chanhassen. MN 55317

Dedication

To Geraldine Jacobsen, the beautiful spirit who taught me
that I'm a medium, and her daughter Tjody.
Also to my husband Brad, of course, and my Aunt Diane.

Acknowledgements

My most sincere thanks to:

All those people who showed the generosity and courage to share their afterlife-communications experiences with my readers and me: Tjody Jacobsen, Laura Kroeten-Bue, Rick & Stephanie Klaers and family, Herb & Peg Rhoden, Linda Abel, Lyn Danielson, and Carole Nelson Douglas. Also, to everyone who shared their experiences anonymously.

To my editor, Jinjer Stanton, who left no stone unturned and no statement unchallenged. Your broad knowledge of all things metaphysical was a great help to me.

And, again, to my longtime friend and bestselling novelist, Carole Nelson Douglas, my sister in this "Authors' Direct" venture. I cannot thank you enough for all the hours of wisdom and encouragement you've given me.

To the spirits of my dead mother, Dorothy, and my dead father, Carl. Thanks for letting me know, in so many little ways, how often you're with me and how much you care.

Finally, to my husband, Brad, for believing in my medium work and my writing abilities long before anyone else did.

Table of Contents

Introduction:
Discovering the Medium Within 1

Chapter 1
Soul Sensing vs. Mediumship:
How I Reconnected a Soul Senser with
Her Passed Loved One........................ 13

Chapter 2
The Signs of Visitation:
What I Taught the Klaers Family to Look For 41

Chapter 3
Why Soul Sensing Works 63

Chapter 4
The Real Barriers:
Those I've Helped Master Their Doubts and Fears........... 73

Chapter 5
Why & How to Protect Yourself:
Lyn's Dead Friend Takes Her for a Ride 89

Chapter 6
Getting Your Right Brain Right:
How I Taught Dr. Laura Kroeten-Bue to Pierce the Veil 105

Chapter 7
Soul Sensing With Your Chakras 127

Chapter 8
Soul Sensing With Your Intuition 147

Chapter 9
Afterlife-Communication Tools and How to Use Them 163

Chapter 10
Monitoring Your Night Dreams:
*What I've Taught Bill and Others about Soul Sensing
in Their Sleep*.. 187

Chapter 11
Observing the Etiquette of Visitation:
*How I Helped Jean & Shelley Reopen the
Communication Channels* *199*

Chapter 12
Encouraging Visitation:
*The Tips I've Shared with My Clients for Attracting the
Souls of Their Loved Ones* *215*

Chapter 13
Communicating with Passed Pets *233*

Chapter 14
Sending Messages and Getting Confirmation *243*

Staying In Touch *258*

INTRODUCTION

Discovering the Medium Within

In 1992, I suddenly discovered I could convey messages to a virtual stranger from her *dead* mother! Moreover, I did so with the kind of accuracy and specificity that it takes most mediums years to develop. So, naturally, I wondered when all of those years of development had taken place. How could I have possessed such a talent and not even realized it until I was in my 30s? Is everyone born with this ability? Or do only a select few have it? To answer these questions, I decided to take account of my life from the very beginning. And what I found may be very much like the experiences you've had with the spirits of your passed loved ones.

For the first two months of my life I had no name. I was just "baby girl Danielson," an underweight, wailing orphan at the University of Minnesota Hospital and, later, a temporary foster home. My impoverished unwed mother gave me up for adoption, then died six weeks later of complications related to tuberculosis and hepatitis.

It was an indisputably tragic start in life, and I could have spent the rest of my days wallowing in it, soaking up sympathy from everyone who would listen. But, sometimes, there's a reason for tragedy. Although none of us may fully understand it, the worst my mother's voice seemed to be saying within me. But I shrugged it off, believing it was only my imagination playing tricks on me.

I would later learn, during my adoption search, that my mother's name was *Dorothy,* she grew up on a Minnesota farm where tornadoes were not uncommon, and that her mom, at least in some photos, resembled the actress who played Auntie Em in *The Wizard of Oz.* No one could ask for more of a triple play than that. That's some excellent spirit messaging! Unfortunately, like most people, I just did not understand that I was being communicated with from the Other Side. Furthermore, I did not yet have legal access to the adoption information that would validate these messages. (This is an example of **telepathic-image communication or clairvoyance.**)

Also in the 80s, my biological mother found a way to express her thoughts to me through someone else's words. The musical *Xanadu* was popularizing a song entitled "Magic." "You have to believe we are magic," the lyrics went. Then they said that nothing could stand in our way and that I should never let my aim stray. Somehow I knew these were the exact words my mom wanted to speak to me. (This is **spirit communication through music**.)

As you'll learn in this book, all of these occurrences with the spirit of my biological mother are classic signs of visitation and communication from the Other Side. And, based on my many years of professional mediumship since, I would be surprised if you have not experienced at least one of these signs yourself. But, chances are, you wrote it off as being just a product of your imagination. Or, maybe, you thought it was only wishful thinking. What you probably didn't realize is that such signs are being observed by thousands of people every day. In fact, they're so widespread that it's impossible for them all to be products of imagination or mere coincidences. As with police-gathered testimonies in criminal cases, the commonalities of these worldwide experiences bear out their authenticity. And I'm confident that the lists of signs

INTRODUCTION

of spirit visitation and communication I'll provide for you in this book are the most extensive you'll find anywhere.

Redefining Death

In my youth, I didn't understand precisely what my deceased mother was trying to tell me. That I was a medium? I had no idea what a *medium* was. That I had become hardwired to Heaven throughout a lifetime of being connected to her in spirit? How was such a thing possible? And even if it were, what were the potentials of such a connection? Who would have believed me back in the 1960s if I'd admitted that I somehow communicated with a dead woman I'd never met?

Being adopted, after all, was supposed to have given me a chance for normalcy: a "regular" kind of life with middle-class parents. But death struck *again* when I was 10 years old. My adoptive father died of lung cancer, leaving me no one but my adoptive mother to raise me. Death had left her abandoned by her husband and me by the only father I would ever know.

"I've never had much luck with parents," I would quip years later to friends. "They always die on me."

Death became my enemy. I both feared and hated it. I'd had to deal with it far too much by the age of 10. And it hadn't been just the death of a pet or a grandparent, like the other kids I knew, but of a mom and a dad—the very people I most needed in order to survive.

Naturally, this made me question the teachings of the Christian faith in which I'd been raised. What kind of God, I wondered, would take a child's parents away permanently? How could God be as benevolent as the Lutheran church claimed and yet leave people to suffer the heartbreak of such losses for the rest of their lives?

The answers to these questions had not yet been revealed to me. Or, perhaps, I knew them in my heart, but not in my head.

I only know that the God I now believe in is far too merciful to leave people bereft. I also know that access to Heaven can be found within each of us. I am vastly happier because of these blessings, and it is my hope you will be, too.

Nevertheless, no one knows better than a medium the extent to which words and religious dogma can get in the way when we're trying to communicate with the Other Side. In one of the most poignant novels ever written on the subject of death, Pulitzer-prize-winning author James Agee addresses the conflict between religious doctrines and afterlife communications. The main character in the book, an elementary-school-aged boy named Rufus Follett, has just lost his father to death in a car accident. Because Rufus is considered by his mother to be too young to attend his father's burial, one of Rufus' uncles later tells him about it. This uncle explains that he's not sure he himself believes in the teachings of the church, but he does share a stunning memory with Rufus. The uncle recounts that, once the coffin was lowered to the bottom of the grave, a brilliantly colored butterfly floated down and landed on the lid of it, precisely at the level of the deceased's heart. As the butterfly's wings fluttered there, it was as if Rufus' father's heart was still beating in some unseen world. This occurrence said more to the uncle than all of the sermons spoken by all of the ministers on earth. With a flicker of colorful wings, the author captured the ineffable essence of immortality. Words did not get in the way of this unmistakable sign from Heaven.

Like Rufus in Agee's novel, I, too, had lost my father to death at a very young age. And, although mankind had already done much to conquer physical pain back then with sedatives and anesthetics, I couldn't help noticing that the emotional pain of losing someone to death seemed pretty much swept under the carpet. Western culture's unspoken message about death became clear to me: "He's gone, so move on."

INTRODUCTION

This was what society was saying to me, but it was not what science and nature seemed to indicate. In fact, as you'll learn in Chapter 3, death (as defined by the sloughing off of a physical body) is a relatively new development on earth. Indeed, eternal life has been the norm for 75% longer than death on our planet. So, should we assume that someone ceases to exist just because they have become disembodied?

On the contrary, not being restricted by a physical body has enabled my biological mother to do many things for and with me that she could never have done in corporeal form. She has forewarned me of upcoming events and communicated with me telepathically for years. And many of my clients report the same kinds of amazing interactions with their loved ones on a weekly or even daily basis. So, instead of going to Heaven permanently and leaving us behind, it appears that many of our deceased loved ones are capable of bringing aspects of Heaven down to us.

Grieve Less by Communicating More

Two months after my father's passing, the boy who lived next door, a frequent playmate of mine, suggested we try communicating with my dad through a Ouija® board. I angrily dismissed the idea, feeling insulted that he thought my relationship with my father could somehow be restored with what is essentially a board game! But I now realize that the intention behind his suggestion had been constructive. The son of a prominent scientist, this boy possessed an inherent curiosity about the world and the natures of life and death. "If people's souls really live on after death," he'd reasoned, "why shouldn't we be able to communicate with them?"

It was an excellent question. Unfortunately, I would not seriously ponder it for another decade or two. My spiritual links to my deceased mom and dad remained intensely private to me. I never spoke of them, because in the time and places in which I found myself, such things were rarely, if ever, discussed.

Nowadays, however, mediumship is one of the most popular topics on TV and radio. It both embraces its roots in ancient China, Egypt, Greece, and the British Isles, and it holds itself to much higher standards than were exhibited during the séances of the late 19th and early 20th Centuries. Documented accuracy and specificity of medium messages have taken the place of parlor tricks and rigged levitations.

And the advances continue. Instead of simply having to wait around for your deceased relatives and friends to communicate with you, this book will enable you to awaken your soul-sensing abilities and give you many ways to encourage spirit communications and visitations. In fact, one of the main reasons why our loved ones in Heaven don't visit us is because we so rarely acknowledge their efforts to do so! Once you read in Chapter 4 of this book about the ways in which Western funeral practices are designed to keep the spirits of our dead away from us, you'll understand that not only have our minds been closed to visitation for centuries, but our homes as well.

Helping the Dead Help Us

In the early 1970s, one of my adoptive grandfathers died of a heart attack. Several minutes later he was revived by a doctor. This grandfather had always been an angry, violent sort. Yet, suddenly, after claiming to have "gone to Heaven" and seen his long-dead wife, he changed his ways dramatically. He became dedicated to his church, and a sweet, never-before-seen side of him emerged.

"There's something to this life-after-death thing," I remember thinking, "if such an experience can turn an all-time nasty drunk like him into someone nice."

Death had transformed this relative, yet I still hated the very mention of the word. On some subtle level, however, the subject of death flirted with me. When I was in high school, I fell in love with Thornton Wilder's play *Our Town*, and, of course, with

INTRODUCTION

James Agee's *A Death in the Family*. And my favorite holiday was and always will be Halloween, a Celtic vigil whose 2,500-year-old roots are founded in the belief of the soul's survival after death.

"You were born on April 30th, weren't you?" one of my New-Age friends asked me when I was in my late twenties.

"Yes. So?"

"So, you might be a conduit to the Other Side. April 30th is the counterpart of October 31st, Halloween—the time of year when the Celts believed the veil between the living and the dead is the thinnest. Both days are considered to be portals in time between the worlds of the living and the dead."

"That's ridiculous," I told him. "If I were ever to acknowledge such an ability, I would certainly want a much more scientific and modern explanation for it. And what a creepy talent, anyway. Who'd want to talk to ghosts?"

Then, like a bolt from the blue, I heard my biological mother retort in my head, "I beg your pardon! I'm not a ghost, I'm an *angel*. We prefer to be called 'angels' or 'spirits.' Not ghosts!" And that was the very first inkling I received of how it must feel to be deceased and trying to maintain ties with the living. I somehow realized in that instant that the dead are insulted, ignored, and forgotten on a regular basis by the very people they're trying to comfort, help, and communicate with on Earth.

How in the world can we hope to have ongoing relationships with our deceased loved ones when we don't give them the respect and sensitivity they deserve? We talk about having "respect for the dead" in Western culture, yet we don't usually practice it beyond the holding of wakes, reviewals, funerals, and the occasional placing of flowers on graves.

National surveys show that up to 86% of those polled in the U.S. believe in some sort of afterlife, but most of our religions teach us that, once a loved one dies, we cannot communicate with or see him or her until we ourselves die. And, in most cases, that's an unmercifully long period of time.

If we cannot communicate with the dead, why am I able to do so for hundreds of clients across the U.S. every year (and with a money-back guarantee of contact, no less)? And why do so many people claim to have been visited by the deceased?

I've found, over my many years of mediumship, that it is not only possible for families and friends to receive messages from their dead loved ones, it's actually *typical*. Most of us are given opportunities for afterlife exchanges without even realizing it. And now that I've learned how difficult it can be for our dead to bring through signs and messages to us, I'm dedicated to making sure you don't overlook those communications. Our deceased loved ones should not have to turn cartwheels just to get our attention. And, far worse, are all the times when they finally have to give up trying to communicate because the living are just too uninformed to use their soul senses and to recognize afterlife messages.

You Don't Have to Say Goodbye!

Some people view mediumship as a means by which to say a final good-bye to a loved one who has passed. I do not. My lifetime of experience in communicating with my dead parents has taught me that many relationships are meant to be ongoing. I probably would not have survived to adulthood without two such caring spirit parents looking out for me and constantly conveying their love and confidence in me. And other true accounts, like the one in this book about the continuous communications between a deceased artist named Peter Bue and his surviving wife, Laura, abound with the many ways in which our dead loved ones continue to be active in our day-to-day lives.

I know some people and religions claim to fear afterlife communications because of the possibility of evil spirits slipping through in the process. But I say, "Why let a few bad apples spoil

INTRODUCTION

this Heavenly gift of connection for us all?" There are some highly effective ways to prevent being bothered by malevolent souls and I'll share them with you in this book. Provided you are specific about whom you want to communicate with and be visited by, you should never be troubled by ghosts or uninvited spirits. As with the previously uncharted cyberspace of the Internet, the advantages of such communications almost always outweigh the risks.

I'm convinced now that we all possess some ability to give and receive messages from those we thought we had lost to death. This book will assist you in identifying and developing your own miraculous soul senses. It will cause you to start noticing significant butterflies. And it will help prove to you that those dearest to you in Heaven are rarely more than a whisper away.

Chapter 1

Soul Sensing vs. Mediumship

*How I Reconnected a Soul Senser
with Her Passed Loved One*

I've had some unusual things happen to me. I've seen a tornado coming right for me. I've been in the driver's seat of a car that was being swept away in a flash flood. I was even struck by lightning in my own home in 1984! But all of those occurrences were due to natural causes, completely explicable in current scientific terms. What happened to me in the spring of 1992 was not.

I was just minding my own business—literally. I'd had some novels released by New York publishers under the penname Ashland Price, and I was under contract to write several more. So, I needed to hire a graphics artist to create promotional materials for my books. I found one named Tjody Jacobsen in my local Yellow Pages, and I called to make an appointment with her. She was running the business out of her home in a suburb of Minneapolis. Upon arriving at her townhouse, I realized I knew its previous owner: a friend named Elaine.

When Tjody greeted me at the door, I immediately noticed how she had redecorated the place in warm Southwestern tones: copper, orange, and tan. It showed an excellent eye for color and accessorizing. I instantly felt comfortable with this 30-ish blond and her broad, disarming smile. Like me, she was short and her last name, like mine, said she was also of Scandinavian descent. But, unlike me, there was an athletic air about her, augmented by a cast on her right leg. She'd broken it in some way she didn't elaborate on, saying only, "Kids will be kids."

I knew at once she would be a breath of fresh air in my sedentary, solitary, book-writing life. The decorating choices she had made in the townhouse told me she was in love with the American West. I, on the other hand, the daughter of an Air Force Colonel who had been stationed in such places as the Philippines and Washington D.C., was much more attuned to the East. *Contrast*, I thought. That's always good in a collaborative relationship.

I told Tjody I'd known the previous owner of her townhouse. She replied that she liked her new home, but wished Elaine had informed her the place was haunted before selling it to her.

"Haunted?" I said with a laugh. "I've been here several times and Elaine never mentioned anything like that."

"It is, though," Tjody maintained. "I hear strange noises at night. And my cat acts like she senses someone else here, even though it's just the two of us."

"Weird. I mean, it's fairly new construction. I think Elaine was the first owner, and she never said a word about any disturbances here."

Frankly, I was almost as surprised by Tjody's candor as I was by her claim. Minnesota isn't the kind of place where people go around talking about hauntings, especially with strangers. Had I been less open-minded, I might have decided that I'd just made the acquaintance of a true eccentric. Instead, I would later conclude that I had met my first "soul senser." That's a term I've coined related to everybody's ability to act as a medium. But, back then, in 1992, I didn't know what a medium was ... even though I was about to discover I was one myself!

Soul Sensing vs. Mediumship

As Tjody led me into her living room, I spotted a framed photograph on the front lid of her piano. It was a picture of a middle-aged woman, and I instantly, inexplicably knew that *she* was responsible for the strange happenings in the townhouse. I said as much to Tjody, and she informed me that the lady in the photo was her mother, who had died six years earlier in a horseback-riding accident.

Then *it* happened: the strangest experience I'd ever had, an invisible, unheralded crossing into another realm that would forever change my life. A voice inside my head said the words "Lady Jane," and, to my astonishment, I uttered them aloud. I stood there dumbfounded, afraid Tjody would think I'd lost my mind.

But she simply looked curious and mildly intrigued. "What?"

I wanted to simply dismiss it, but something made me plunge ahead. "It's like your mother is talking to me, in my head. And she says, 'Lady Jane.' Who is that?"

Tjody immediately started to cry. "My God," she exclaimed. "That was my mom's nickname for me. I haven't heard it in ages."

I was even more stunned than she was. I had just relayed the words of a person I'd never met—a woman who had died six years earlier! I was in Tjody's parlor, yet I knew for a fact that there were no "parlor tricks" involved. There was nothing up my sleeve, absolutely no way I could know what I did about this stranger's mother.

If Tjody shared any of my incredulity, she didn't show it. She just seemed anxious to have me communicate as many messages from her mom as possible, before my baffling ability vanished.

I understood, firsthand, how she felt, because I had lost both my biological mother and adoptive father to death by the time I was 10. I knew how strong the bond between parents and their kids can be.

"What else is she telling you?" she asked, continuing to look intrigued.

"Ducks. She's talking about *ducks*. What's that mean?"

Tjody thought for a moment. "Well, I had a pet duck when I was little. And one of the first toys I remember receiving was a rubber duck. I still have it, in fact."

I silently noted that Tjody's mother was bringing through memories. "Now, she's saying her first name ends with an 'een' sound. Something like 'Marlene' or 'Darlene?'"

Tjody smiled. "Geraldine."

"And she played the piano?"

"Yes. This piano was hers."

I laughed at the next thing that popped into my head. "She says that talking through me is like playing an untuned piano." I imagine Geraldine was right about that. I'd never before intentionally attempted spirit communication. My only frame of reference was the Gypsy séances I'd seen in movies—those ridiculous scenes with tables levitating and strange voices issuing from a channeler.

So, *what* was happening now? After thirty-odd years of life, it was like I had discovered I could fly without aid of an airplane. And I had to admit to myself that, if what I was experiencing was truly some sort of "possession," it was one of the most uplifting, soul-cleansing experiences I'd ever had. My impression of Geraldine was that she was pure, heavenly love, an angelic being. She obviously adored her daughter and that reverent energy was flowing freely through me.

I continued to convey her messages to Tjody. "She says there was a gelatin salad she used to make for your family's Christmas dinner. It was red with a cinnamon flavor to it. She says some of you didn't like it. There was always a dustup at the Christmas dinner table because you wouldn't eat it."

"That's right. My father would get mad at us about not cleaning our plates."

"And she put whipped cream in the center of the Jello® ring?"

"No. Around the rim of it."

"She keeps showing me images of flower gardens, but they're in a range of colors I can barely comprehend. There's a crystal cathedral in the background and it's covered in bright light, inside and out. It's like she's showing me snapshots of Heaven, as if she wants you to see all that she's seeing."

Tjody was silent for a few seconds. "I'll bet it's because we gave her eyes away."

"What?"

"We made her an organ donor after she died. And her eyes are some of the organs we gave away."

"She wants you to know she can see again. She has eyes again in Heaven," I deduced. I was deeply moved by this revelation. What a tremendous comfort and gift it could be to organ-donors' families everywhere.

"O.K. Now she's showing me a gingerbread house, which somehow says 'Germany' to me. Was she German?"

"Yes. Mostly. But she was English, too. She always referred to herself as a 'Heinz 57.' But I know she wanted to visit Germany. She never got the chance to, though."

"Maybe that's what she's referring to."

I realized this was a trickier process than I had thought. Words I could hear through some sort of telepathy were being intermingled with images that might have been exact or might merely have symbolized something else. I decided to just tell Tjody everything I was receiving and let her help me interpret the meanings.

"You say she died in a riding accident?"

"Yes. In Montana."

"She's saying the name 'Pat.' Who is that?"

"My aunt, the person she was visiting when she had her accident."

I started to feel as touched and tearful as Tjody. I'm not much of a crier, having been raised by stoic Swedish-Americans, but the love Geraldine felt for her daughter, coupled with her great joy at being able to communicate with Tjody again was overwhelming. Whatever was happening was deeply spiritual, like nothing I'd ever experienced. It seemed to lift my soul to rapturous heights, even though my body was, by this time, firmly planted on this new acquaintance's sofa.

Tjody now sounded both anxious and perplexed. "Ask her why she went horseback riding before my husband and I got out there. We were on our way to join her in Montana the very next day. Why didn't she wait until we arrived?"

"I don't want to lay blame here, but she says your Aunt Pat urged her to go riding at that point."

I paused, still unable to see the accident itself. (I've since learned that many spirits don't like talking about their manner of death. Passing away is rarely pleasant, after all. So, I can understand their reluctance to mar the splendor of Heaven with talk of the physical distress of dying). "What happened, Tjody? Do you know how she died exactly?"

"They were riding over a stone bridge and the horses were spooked by some government equipment there. They turned and ran away at full speed. Mom fell backwards off her horse and hit her head on that stone surface of the bridge. She slipped into a coma and was taken to a hospital where she later died without regaining consciousness..." Tjody's voice broke off in tears.

"But she wants you to know that at least this was a fairly quick and painless death. She knows now that, had she not passed in this accident, she would have died a far more painful and lingering death from cancer or lung disease."

"Yes. I've thought that, too. We think she probably already had emphysema because she smoked quite a bit."

"Then, I guess it was better this way, even though you didn't get to say your good-byes. You're saying them now, through me, I think. She's letting us know that her spirit is still very much alive and well."

"Does she think I was right to get a divorce?"

"She says, 'Yes.' You were unhappy in your marriage."

"That's true," Tjody agreed. "And does she think it's good that I've started my own business?"

"Yes."

"Can she tell me anything more?"

"You have more than one brother?"

"Two."

"She seems worried about your youngest brother. Something about his little finger."

"Yes. He was doing some carpentry work at home last weekend and he had an accident with a saw. He cut off his little finger. But the doctors were able to reattach it and it looks like it will be O.K."

"She says to tell this brother to please be more careful. And the same goes for you with your broken leg. She says you could get hurt in a car accident. Do you understand?"

She nodded. "I guess I've been taking some risks I shouldn't."

I suggested this might be why her mother had been "haunting" the place, hoping desperately to make her daughter hear her.

I've since come to realize that many of our departed loved ones are trying to guide and caution us, but we often don't hear their messages. It was just by sheer chance that Geraldine and I were able to communicate with Tjody that day. What a shame it is that so many of our deceased relatives and friends are driven to poltergeist-like activity in order to get our attention.

"Can you tell me something I can pass on to my dad?" Tjody asked. "I know he really misses Mom, but I don't think he'd believe in this type of thing, unless you tell me something that only he and Mom would know."

I strained to receive any secret detail Geraldine could give me about her husband. "Green bedroom," I said finally. "What does it mean?" I asked Tjody. "Did your parents have a green bedroom at any point?"

"Not that I know of."

I tried to interpret this further. "Could your mom be referring to a camping trip or some time when your parents slept outdoors? Could 'green' symbolize nature?"

"Well, they did spend their honeymoon on a dude ranch."

"Where they slept in a tent or outside?"

"No. In a bunkhouse. But that's pretty much out in the open, like a barn."

"Your mother says she found it embarrassing. There wasn't much privacy there for newlyweds. I guess you could tell your father this and see if he remembers her acting self-conscious, because, clearly, this is a memory that just the two of them shared."

"Right. I'll ask the next time I talk to him. What about my nieces? Does Mom know that one of them is in the Hopkins Raspberry Queen contest?"

I was struck by how down to earth this question was. It snapped me out of the heightened sensations I'd been experiencing and I knew I was definitely straddling two worlds.

"I can't tell if she knows this. She simply shows me two little blond girls and says they are her granddaughters. She feels great love for them. Perhaps she's showing them to me as they were when she died."

"That was six years ago. So they were very young back then."

I started to feel tired and I sensed that Geraldine's connection with me was fading. Even though it seemed I'd only been communicating with her for a few minutes, I glanced at my watch and was shocked to see that nearly an hour had passed. As with my creative writing, this spirit communication experience seemed to blank out my perception of time. I was later to discover why. I was later to discover *a lot* of things about mediumship.

For the time being, however, I explained to Tjody that I could no longer hear her mother's voice and that I was feeling strangely worn out. Tjody suggested that I try communicating with Geraldine again some time, perhaps with Tjody's brothers and father present.

I agreed, but wasn't sure this otherworldly connection could ever be re-established. Then I went over my advertising project with Tjody, left it with her for completion and drove home in a kind of daze. I felt more like I was flying than driving. I was intensely aware of the blue sky above me and only vaguely sensing the highway on which I was traveling.

My own happy accident of discovering my medium abilities had somehow linked up with Geraldine Jacobsen's fatal accident of six years earlier. Yet, due to several pressing book deadlines, many months would pass without my using this talent again or even learning that those of us who possess it are called "mediums."

Soul Sensing versus Mediumship

A medium is a living person who is able to communicate with the spirits of the dead. But I probably wouldn't have realized I could receive messages from Tjody's deceased mom, if Tjody hadn't made me aware that a spirit was present in her new townhome. I did not initially sense that Tjody was being visited by someone from the Other Side. It was Tjody herself who was first aware of it. And she detected this with nothing more than her bodily senses. She said she had been *hearing* strange noises at night and she had *seen* her cat acting as though some invisible being was present. So they were the ones who laid the groundwork for my initial foray into doing afterlife communications for others. They became aware there was a soul present and that fact made them "soul sensers,"— the name I've since given to those with this very widespread ability.

A Broader Range of Senses

Animals, like Tjody's cat, possess more acute physical senses than humans do. The average dog, for instance, can detect sounds at a higher and wider range than people can. Sensory testing indicates that canine hearing is nearly 30,000 cycles per second higher than ours. The sounds produced by dog whistles, virtually inaudible to the human ear, can be heard from quite a distance by our beloved pooches. This is why family pets are often the first in a household to become aware of a visiting spirit.

Animals are not only capable of hearing better and farther than we can, it appears they're also able to hear *faster*. When paranormal investigators record EVPs (Electronic Voice Phenomena) on tape, it often indicates that spirit speech is emitted at twice the speed of the human ear's ability to listen to it. In other words, recordings of EVPs usually need to be slowed down two times for the living to hear and comprehend them. Spirit orbs and images, invisible to the naked eye, are frequently captured on film in the instant the camera's shutter opens and closes. All of this explains the contention by many mediums and ghost hunters that disembodied souls exist at a faster and higher vibration than the living. So, **just because we cannot hear, see, feel, or smell something, does not mean it's not present.**

Even if you sense the presence of a disembodied soul, you may not know why he or she is visiting. Tjody and her cat didn't know who was visiting or why. I, the accidental medium, had to help them identify and communicate with their invisible caller. That's where most full-fledged mediums enter the picture. They bring through information that identifies the visiting spirit and helps explain the reason for his or her presence.

Soul Sensing vs. Mediumship

Sometimes the reason is as simple as the availability of a medium. Often, when I offer my services free of charge to one of my relatives or friends who is mourning a passed loved one, that individual will start to experience unexplained and mysterious occurrences. These episodes usually continue *until* he or she has a session with me. Once this medium appointment takes place, the strange happenings typically cease. Apparently, when their dead loved ones have had their opportunity to communicate, there is no need for them to continue exhibiting conspicuous signs of visitation.

Mediums Are Born

How are professional mediums able to hear the messages of the dead? Most of them possess an extrasensory hearing ability called "clairaudience." Even if a medium is physically deaf, he or she has an inner or hidden ability to hear without the use of ears. This is called "mental" mediumship because it is contained within the medium's mind. It's the most publicized and prevalent type of mediumship today. But it's certainly not the only kind.

In the 1860s and 1870s, "trance" mediums, also known as "channelers" were most in demand. Audiences and séance participants were fascinated by seeing the trance medium's consciousness give way to a possessing spirit. Changes in voice, word choices, speech patterns, and physical behaviors indicated that another soul had entered the channeler's body. The information received had to be transcribed because the medium often had no memory of it after the session.

While trance mediumship, for the purpose of channeling the dead, is not particularly popular these days, it must be noted that many bestselling books have been written in the past several years by authors claiming to have been possessed by spirits who convey knowledge and wisdom from Heaven. At this point in my career, I prefer to stick with communicating with souls whose past existences on Earth can be documented. But, perhaps, readers feel that the proof of Other-World origin rests in the content of these channeled books. Many see them as a source of revealed wisdom.

Then there's the "physical" medium, who physically manifests visiting spirits. The souls they bring forth manipulate energy systems here on earth. These mediums may materialize spirit bodies or manifest objects from an unseen dimension.

All mediums are psychic and are descendants of the earliest shamans, so they can often trace their extrasensory talents along their family trees. These gifts date back at least 50,000 years to the first Neanderthals, who needed psychic abilities to help locate animals to eat, drinkable water, and safe caves to inhabit. Such extrasensory perception was crucial to the survival of the human race back then. So, those with shamans in their tribes or clans had the evolutionary advantage. This seems to account for the widespread presence today of psychics, mediums, and spiritual healers amongst all populations around the world.

Soul Sensers Are Developed

Everyone, not just mediums, possesses nonphysical senses. I call them "soul" senses, because I think they constitute some of the best evidence that we all have souls. But they are also called "astral" (out-of-body) senses. They are what we use to perceive information when we are in a dream phase of sleep or when we're out of our bodies. These senses operate at such a high speed, however, that, when we detect stimuli with them, we have trouble registering the information they provide. We are, therefore, apt to write this experience off merely as a product of our imaginations.

Let's say, for instance, that you're all alone and you suddenly catch an unexplained whiff of your long-dead grandmother's perfume. This ability is called "clairalience." Or, you're driving past the street on which your deceased uncle used to live, and, out of the corner of your eye, you glimpse a bearded figure who looks just like him. This is "clairvoyance." (When used in the mediumistic sense, this term refers to the ability to see the dead and/or the images they wish to convey to us.)

Again, these perceptions usually happen so quickly that they are easily dismissed as sheer imaginings; yet they are as real as any information you gather with your five physical senses.

Your Seven Soul Senses

The soul senses include:

1. **Clairvoyance**—(**"Clear seeing"**): the ability to see disembodied souls and/or the images they wish to convey.

2. **Clairaudience**—(**"Clear hearing"**): hearing the voices and thoughts of souls.

3. **Clairsentience**—(**"Clear feeling"**): feeling sensations, emotions, or the sentiments instilled by a soul.

4. **Clairsentinence**—(**"Clear consciousness or clear watching"**): correctly determining the physical problems or ailments a soul suffered before he or she died. (This ability is common in spiritual healers.)

5. **Clairalience**—(**"Clear smelling"**): smelling scents associated with a soul when he or she was alive, such as cigarette smoke or a particular perfume or aftershave.

6. **Clairgustance**—(**"Clear tasting"**): receiving taste impressions from a soul.

7. **Claircognizance** (**"Clear knowing"**): knowing, with mysterious certainty, whether a message from the spirit realm is accurate or inaccurate. This sense also includes other types of knowing, such as being able to determine who is trying to communicate with you from the Other Side and an awareness

of whether you are simply being visited by a spirit or actually haunted by a ghost.

Visitations versus Hauntings

As a general rule, we are *visited* by those we have known in our current lifetimes, such as deceased relatives, friends, and pets. The term "haunting," on the other hand, tends to apply to having our homes and lives trespassed upon by spirits who are strangers to us. This, by extension, means that, if you are being haunted, you probably won't be able to figure out why—at least not without the help of a medium or detailed historic records about your setting. Hauntings also differ from visitations in that they often have a threatening aspect to them. True visitation, by contrast, almost always feels benevolent or harmless in nature.

Before Tjody learned from me that she was being visited by her deceased mother, she concluded her townhouse was haunted. There are two reasons why she thought this. Firstly, she had just moved into the townhome and had never experienced paranormal happenings before, so she naturally assumed the presence she was perceiving was due to her new location. Secondly, her mother had died six years earlier, so Tjody didn't associate this spirit visitation with her mom.

In most cases, though, visitation by a passed loved one takes place within hours to months after said death, making it fairly easy to figure out who's visiting. Usually, the spirit is simply trying to confirm for you that his or her soul has survived physical death.

Put yourself in your deceased loved one's spot for a moment and you'll quickly understand why it's so important to the dead to get their message of soul survival across to the living. Suppose you had gotten caught in the December 2004 Indian Ocean tsunami, but you had physically survived it. Wouldn't you want to contact some of your family members, friends, or coworkers

Soul Sensing vs. Mediumship

to inform them you didn't perish in the disaster? With phone lines and other communication systems destroyed by the tsunami, wouldn't you try to get the message of your survival to your loved ones in any other way you could? ... Of course. And that is precisely what our deceased family members and friends are trying to do after they die. What's more, they'll often go to great lengths to succeed with it.

A few years ago, my brother-in-law, Herb, lost an older brother named John to a sudden heart attack. I offered to do a free medium session for Herb, not only to console him, but because I had not known his brother well enough for my medium work to be compromised in this case. Herb and his wife, Peg, were gracious about my offer, but, leading busy lives, they let a couple months pass before taking me up on it.

By that time, John's spirit had caused three telekinetic events to take place in their home. It was clear John wasn't willing to go unacknowledged by them much longer. The first night of his visitation, John woke Herb and Peg in the middle of the night with the sound of something crashing to the floor in their bedroom. What fell was never determined, but the experience naturally startled them.

On the second night, John's visitation was more subtle, but equally alarming. (It often takes the dead a little practice to hone their signals to the living.) This time, the couple's clock radio suddenly emitted a blue light that illuminated their entire bedroom and again woke both of them from deep sleep.

By this point, John had fully captured Herb and Peg's attention. They could have written off these unusual occurrences as mere coincidences or chance happenings, but they'd heard enough about spirit visitation from me through the years not to do so.

John's next step was to provide a sign that identified himself as their visitor. Like Herb, he'd been a gun collector in life. So, he chose this commonality to put his spiritual "signature" on his visits. He did this by cocking one of the guns in Herb's collection case.

Anyone who collects guns knows better than to leave one cocked. Herb, an army firearms trainer, would certainly never do anything so careless. And Peg, the only other person living in their house, wouldn't dream of touching her husband's prized collection of guns. Nevertheless, Herb found one of them cocked just a couple of days after the clock-radio incident.

He immediately recognized it as John's calling card. John had served in the U.S. Army as well and had a similar interest in antique and modern-day guns. He knew that many people would have passed by their gun cases without noticing this potentially perilous development, but Herb was far too vigilant about such things to miss it.

Herb and Peg scheduled a medium appointment with me shortly thereafter, and, after the session, the signs of visitation stopped at their house. During our session, John came through with information that he and Herb had not shared with another living soul. It was clear, beyond a doubt, who had been visiting them and trying to communicate from the Other Side.

When my long-time friend, Helen, died in Arizona in 2004, she left her calling card in an even more precise way. I was informed of her sudden death during a long-distance call from Helen's daughter a couple days after her burial, and I was very sad that I had missed her funeral. However, Helen was kind enough to offer me some closure by giving me physical signs of her visitation that I could not miss. Because I'm a medium, she could have simply tried to send me some telepathic messages. But, since I receive scores of these for my clients every week, it was more effective for Helen's signs to come to me in a very physical way. She obliged by knocking down two of the gifts she had given me over the years. One of these presents was a Native-American wind chime, which inexplicably fell seven feet to my patio without damaging its ceramic bells! The other was a photograph of her, which had been affixed to a bulletin board in my home office. Her photo was surrounded by those of several of my other friends, but only Helen's fell in that breeze-less setting. Her message was unmistakable: "Hello. It's me, Helen. I'm sorry I didn't get the chance to say goodbye to you before I died. But I am with you now." To this day, I still marvel at what a good friend she was to bring me such specific solace.

Determining Who's Visiting

If, like Tjody, however, you're not sure whose soul is visiting, you can further your soul-sensing process by answering these questions.

1. **Which of your family members, friends, or pets has most recently died?**

   In most cases, the loved one who died last is visiting you.

2. **What signs of visitation are you receiving via your five bodily senses?**

3. **What signs of visitation are you receiving through your soul senses?**

   a. Are you catching sight of a disembodied spirit? (Clairvoyance) If so, can you identify him or her? (You may need to look through old family photo albums in order to recognize an ancestor who's visiting you. This most commonly applies to children in your household who claim to be seeing spirits. In Chapter 3, I'll explain why kids are much more likely than adults to see passed loved ones.)

   b. Are you inwardly hearing the voice of or phrases used by a deceased loved one? (Clairaudience)

   c. Are you feeling sensations, emotions, or sentiments you associate with a dead family member, friend, or pet?

(Clairsentience) Pay close attention to your chakras: the seven energy centers located along your body. These include the crown of your head, your forehead, throat area, solar plexus, abdomen, and hips. If you feel mysterious tingling sensations around your throat and shoulders, for instance, the spirit visiting you is very likely someone who was not only close to you emotionally, but with whom you shared similar thoughts and beliefs. If you feel a warm sensation near your heart or solar plexus, your relationship with this spirit was probably filled with love and warm emotion, but was not particularly cerebral in nature. (This is common with a passed pet.)

d. Are you feeling or sensing the physical condition of a loved one before he or she died? (Clairsentinence) Although clairsentinence is usually associated with those who possess healing abilities, many people report feeling phantom chest pain while or soon after a friend or relative suffered a fatal heart attack, or dizziness when a loved one died from a stroke. Again, these empathic sensations can help you determine who is visiting you.

e. Are you catching whiffs of a deceased loved one's cigarette smoke, perfume, or shaving cologne, when none of these substances are physically in your environment? (Clairalience) This is a classic calling card from the Other Side, and it can help you deduce which soul is visiting.

f. Are you suddenly experiencing the taste of your grandmother's ginger cookies or her other secret recipes, even though she's been dead for years? (Clairgustance) If so, it's pretty likely she's checking in with you. Again, this is an inward sense, not the same as physically tasting a meal you've prepared for yourself, for instance.

g. Do you simply *know* about things you haven't learned through the physical information sources in your life? (Claircognizance) For instance, have you ever known about a death in your family or circle of friends *before* you were told about it? This is known as "presaging" death and indicates that your soul-sensing abilities are unusually strong. You may even be an actual medium. Knowing anything about a deceased loved one's passing that you couldn't possibly have learned through your bodily senses is proof that claircognizance is your strong suit. Fortunately for you, those with "clear knowing" can trust their guts when it comes to determining who's visiting them from the afterlife and why.

4. Can you find any "calling card" or "signature" in the visitation?

John cocked a gun in order to identify himself to his brother Herb. My friend Helen knocked down two of the gifts she'd given me within a few days after her death. What a spirit chooses to disturb or move often has his or her identity written all over it.

5. Have your recent emotions been calling a deceased loved one?

Human emotions play a key role in paranormal happenings. Spirits are often attracted by our feelings, even if we aren't fully aware of the emotions we're emitting. This is why so many people report sensing the presence of "guardian angels" when they find themselves in sudden danger, such as a car accident. The fear and shock we feel in such awful circumstances are like a fire alarm to our loved ones on the Other Side. This explains why Geraldine Jacobsen's visit to her daughter took six years to occur. Tjody had entered a turbulent and highly emotional phase of her life. When I met her, she had recently divorced, broken her leg in a fall, started a freelance business, and moved into a new townhouse. These events were major transitions riddled with doubt and anxiety.

Tjody later told me she felt depressed at that time and was taking unnecessary risks and acting carelessly, as her broken leg indicated. With just two brothers and an aging father left in her family, she felt she had lost the one person in her immediate family in whom she could truly confide: her mother. On some level, Tjody had been beckoning her mom's spirit for months before I showed up on her doorstep. She had already deduced that a spirit had joined her in her new home, she just needed a little help with the identification process.

Your emotions can act as a spiritual magnet, so ask yourself who they are attracting to you.

Asking For the Spirit You Want

Not only can our dead loved ones leave calling cards for us, but we can do the same for them. Here's how:

1. **Ask for the person by name.** The ancient Egyptians, who knew a thing or two about the quest for immortality, had a proverb that read: "To speak the name of the dead is to make them live again." Any professional medium can tell you there's truth to that. Dead or alive, we're all programmed to answer to our names. What's more, anonymity is never advisable when it comes to afterlife communications. You could be inviting spirits into your life who are negative or predatory, so always speak the name of the soul you seek.

2. **Ask for a visit aloud, when you're alone.** It's no coincidence that most people report experiencing spirit visitation when they're alone—in a car, out in the garden, or when they're the last to leave the office at the end of a workday, for instance. It's much easier for the dead to establish contact with us when we're in a quiet, undistracted state. So, those are the times to

ask for visitation from the loved one with whom you want to communicate. Although some souls are capable of reading our thoughts, others seem to require a physically audible form of communication. Even if it's only in a whisper, address the spirit by name and ask for a visit. If you need their guidance, affection, or just their company for a while, simply ask for it. It may take a day or two before your deceased loved one visits, but, most of the time, he or she will come through for you—either when you're awake or in a dreaming phase of sleep.

3. **Back your request with emotion.** What do you feel when you think of your passed relative, friend, or pet? Love? Grief? Longing for his or her company? Whatever it is, don't just feel it, *express* it. Say out loud, "I miss you. I need you. I must have your help right now with this decision I'm trying to make."

Emotion creates the energy required to expand the channels between the living and the dead. That's why you need to ignore any grief counseling that suggests you "stuff" your sorrow and other emotions and "just get on with your life." If you open your feelings to Heaven, you'll receive the healing communications you need. And this will help you get on with your life a whole lot sooner than trying to deny what you feel.

Gathering Identifying Information

The first step in a professional medium session is receiving identifying information from the spirit in question. As a soul senser, this should be your first step too. Afterlife communications should never be treated as a "parlor game" that starts with, "Is there anyone on the Other Side who would like to talk to me?" That's like flinging your front door open and inviting strangers into your home. If this were not a dangerous practice, we wouldn't need locks on our doors. So, it's best to play it safe and determine whom you're talking to in the spirit world.

A good way to start this process is with a pendulum or locket necklace. It's very rare for the deceased to move anything heavy, so the object you use for afterlife communications should be lightweight. A pendulum or a necklace with a locket on it can offer a spirit the opportunity to provide "yes" or "no" answers to your questions. For instance, you might ask, "Mom, is that you?" Then the spirit can give you an affirmative or negative reply.

For further identification, try more complicated "yes/no" questions to which you're sure only a specific dead loved one will know the answers, like "Mom, was your favorite color purple?" (When you're certain her favorite color was actually green).

1. Prop an elbow on a level, solid surface, like a table or a desk.

2. Using the hand propped over the solid surface, hold the pendulum's chain between your forefinger and thumb.

3. Let the chain and pendulum or locket dangle freely, where it won't bump into anything when it starts to swing.

4. Ask your yes/no question aloud and hold the chain as still as possible.

5. If the pendulum begins to swing towards you, then away from you, like the nodding of a head, the spirit is answering "yes" to your inquiry.

6. If the pendulum or locket begins to swing side to side, like the shaking of a head, it's saying "no."

7. If it moves in a diagonal or circular motion, this can be interpreted as "maybe" or "I don't know." (But I'll caution you again at this point that, if you're not getting clear answers as to the identity of your visitor, you should stop your efforts to communicate.) Just as with an Internet chat room, anonymity is the friend of predators, not the benevolent.

8. Be sure to tell the spirit you wish to contact what the different directions of the pendulum's swing will mean to you. Simply say this aloud: "A side-to-side swing means 'no.' A back-and forward swing means 'yes.' A diagonal or circular motion means 'you don't know' or 'you don't understand the question.'" Not all spirits can read our minds, so it's best to speak these instructions out loud.

9. Please note that your pendulum may require several seconds to change directions between the questions you ask, so give it enough time to show a definitive new swing.

In any case, this is the method of pendulum use I recommend for beginning soul sensers, but you may also want to pick up a book on the subject of pendulum reading to learn other ways of using this communication tool. I certainly advocate pendulum use over a Ouija® board. This is because the Ouija board, referred to as a "board game" by its manufacturers, is not, in my opinion, an efficient means of communication with those in the afterlife. Said to require two living participants, the planchette on a Ouija board can give a yes/no answer fairly quickly, but it takes a long time to spell out longer messages. And this, I assure you, is not only trying for the living, but unspeakably tedious for the dead—who, we've established, function at a much higher speed than we do. That's why the next method of spirit communication I recommend is the use of full-color picture cards.

It's in the Cards

Whenever I encounter a situation in which one of my client's loved ones won't speak to me through my clairaudience or clairvoyance (a situation which occurs in about one out of every fifty medium sessions I do), I turn to the Rider Waite tarot deck for help. Most of the time, these communication tools help me bring through identifying information about the spirit my client seeks. I have to say at this point that there is nothing evil about such cards, any more than a pendulum or locket necklace is inherently evil. They are simply communication tools to be used with respect and appropriate caution.

As a soul senser, you too can use tarot cards to gather identifying information from a deceased loved one, and you can do so without being familiar with tarot decks. All you need to do is:

1. Shuffle the cards three times.

2. Fan them out, face-down in front of you.

3. Ask the spirit you seek for identifying information.

4. Turn over a card to which you feel drawn.

5. Look at the images on the card and list any identifying information you see.

The dead tend to be literalists, so don't expect to find a lot of hidden meaning in the cards they lead you to draw. They also tend to describe themselves as they were in the primes of their lives—late 20s through 30s generally. So, even if he or she died with grey or white hair, an earlier hair color is likely to be referenced.

I did this recently for a client who wanted to speak to her dead mother. I couldn't get her mom to identify herself to me through my clairaudience, and she wouldn't show me mental images of herself or her physical traits. So, I pulled a card from the Rider Waite deck. It was The Sun card.

The main figure on The Sun card is blond, so I asked my client, "Was your mother blonde?"

"Yes."

The yellow rays of the sun depicted on this card, against the blue of the sky reminded me of the colors on the Swedish flag, so I followed this hunch. "Was your mother of Scandinavian descent?"

"Yes. She was half Swedish."

Because the main figure on the card is riding a horse, I asked, "Was she athletic? An equestrian, maybe?"

"Yes. She loved horses."

That's three for three, I thought. So, I was pretty sure we could begin our medium session. But, just to be extra certain I had the right spirit on the line, I asked one more identifying question. The main figure pictured on the card is wearing what appears to be a feathered hat. "Was your mother into fashion or dressing up?"

My client smiled and nodded.

Her mom's identity was established and all with just the surface images that happened to catch my eye on the face of a single card. As I said, the dead favor objective information when it comes to identifying themselves. It may take you two or three cards to confirm as much information as I did with just one in this reading. But, whether with a single card or more, this spirit had given me a lot of specific identifying information within just a couple minutes: "In life, I was blonde and Swedish. I liked horses and wore fashionable clothes." So, you should not need much time or an in-depth knowledge of the cards in order to confirm the identity of the spirit with whom you're communicating.

In later chapters, we'll study more complex meanings in the cards as they apply to afterlife conversations. But for now, establishing a spirit's identity should be your only goal. **Again, anonymity is not good when it comes to spirit communication.** So, if, after drawing one or two cards, you cannot identify who is visiting you or the party with whom you wish to speak, it's best to stop your efforts for a few days. It's possible the spirit you seek is otherwise occupied and unable to reply at this time. It's also possible you are a very left-brained person and will need to make an extra effort to become more right-brained and develop your soul senses, as is covered in depth in Chapter 6.

No matter where you are in your soul-sensing development, however, this book will not only teach you how to converse with your deceased loved ones, but how to stay in touch with them on an ongoing basis!

Soul-Sensing Summary

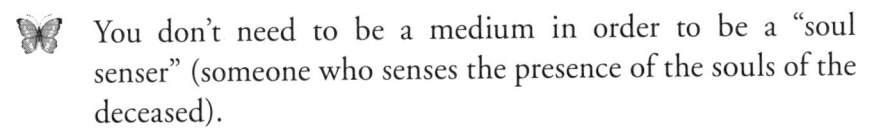

- You don't need to be a medium in order to be a "soul senser" (someone who senses the presence of the souls of the deceased).

- Everyone possesses at least a few of these seven soul senses and they can be honed: clairvoyance (clear seeing), clairaudience (clear hearing), clairsentience (clear feeling), clairsentinence (clear consciousness or clear watching), clairalience (clear smelling), clairgustance (clear tasting), and claircognizance (clear knowing).

- Our soul senses function at a faster speed than our five bodily senses do. This is why the information we gather with them is often dismissed as mere imaginings or coincidences.

- There are big differences between being haunted by a ghost and being visited by one of your dead loved ones.

- Your emotions are an essential part of asking for visitation from a deceased relative, friend, or pet.

- In most cases, you do not need to be a medium to determine who is visiting you or trying to communicate with you from the Other Side.

- Always firmly establish the identity of a loved one before trying to communicate further with him or her. As in an Internet chat room, anonymity favors predators, not the benevolent.

Chapter 2

The Signs of Visitation

What I Taught the Klaers Family to Look For

Imagine all of this: a friend of many years, who has never been demonstrative, greets you with a hug and a kiss on the cheek. The lights in your living room mysteriously dim, then return to their normal wattage seconds later. Your son-in-law, usually the silent type, begins talking a lot and joking with everyone, using the precise words, phrases, and gestures you would expect from another family member. You are inexplicably awakened at 3:00 a.m. several times in one week. When you mention this to a few of your friends, they reveal that this is happening to them as well.

You cannot get your coffeemaker to turn on, even though you've confirmed it's plugged into an electrical outlet and there are no other problems apparent with it. Seconds later, your daughter enters your kitchen and is able to turn on your coffeemaker with ease, despite the fact that she has never used it. You take a break from writing a document on your word processor. When you return to it, someone else has typed a sentence onto your computer screen, even though you are completely alone in the house. You smell your brother's brand of men's cologne wafting past you, but he's not present and neither is anyone else.

Could any of these occurrences be dismissed as being just a product of your imagination? The last one, perhaps; but the rest seem tangible and documentable.

Could any of these strange happenings be simply coincidental? A few of them probably could be. But, when you consider that *all* of these incidents took place within just one week, an unmistakable pattern emerges. You're forced to conclude that an unseen entity has entered your life and it's not only affecting your home's electrical systems, but the behavior of the *people* around you.

Does this sound like the plot from the latest Hollywood horror flick? Stranger than fiction, all of this and more happened to the Richard Klaers family of Minnesota in December of 2006. And, if I hadn't taught them about this language of the dead, they would have missed out on the most precious gift in the world to them at that time: the goodbye messages from their murdered son Greg. It's important to remember, however, that you cannot fully decipher these signs without the background information on each of them.

The Back Stories

Three days before Christmas of 2006, Greg Klaers was stabbed to death while working as a security guard. He was the son of one of my husband's high-school friends. I was standing at our dining-room table wrapping holiday gifts when the phone rang. My husband, Brad, answered and it was our friend Dave calling with the devastating news of Greg's murder. I remember moaning with grief when Brad told me about it.

Greg was only twenty-four years old, and the few encounters I'd had with him had filled me with great affection for him. Like his parents, he was tall, blond, and blue-eyed. He was funny, kind, and, despite his brawny exterior, extremely gentle with kids and animals. In fact, he was so well-liked in his community that some 700 people attended his funeral. He died in the line of duty and received such a hero's honors that his family was inundated with flowers and catered-food deliveries from their friends, extended family, and neighbors for weeks after his death.

Although I didn't know exactly how his parents felt about medium work, I felt strangely compelled to give them messages from their son. To my relief, I began receiving them within just a few hours of Greg's death. One of the first things he told me, with great urgency, was where he had hidden the still-unwrapped Christmas presents he'd bought for his family. (This hiding place was later confirmed by one of his siblings.)

As I entered the Klaers' suburban home with my husband on the morning of Greg's death, the first thing I noticed was their Christmas tree, which Greg had helped decorate. Towering almost all the way up to the peak of their living-room's cathedral ceiling, it was adorned from trunk to top with every color of ornament imaginable. The house, like a festive scene in a snow globe, was now enveloped by the invisible shroud of tragedy that had so suddenly fallen over it.

My husband and I proceeded to the kitchen where Greg's dad, Rick, was sitting at the table, pale with shock and grief. One of Greg's aunts stood near him. She greeted us, her blond hair, round face, and glasses immediately telling me she was from Rick's side of the family. She showed us where to set the deli food we'd brought for Rick and Stephanie. Those of Scandinavian and German descent, like my husband and me, tend not to express their sympathy with shows of physical affection, but with gifts of food. So that's why what happened next shocked me.

Greg's mother, Stephanie, entered the kitchen and without question or pause, I not only hugged her, but I kissed her left cheek. I had known Stephanie Klaers for thirty years. Perhaps I'd greeted her with a hug once or twice in all that time; but I'm simply not demonstrative enough to kiss anyone, except my husband or dog, on the face.

"I don't know why I did that," I mumbled bewilderedly.

"It was because of Greg," she replied tearfully, knowing that I'm a medium. "He usually kissed me on the cheek before leaving for work each evening. But last night I wouldn't let him. We'd had an argument and I was still mad at him."

So, Greg had channeled through me in the instant it took me to kiss his mother's cheek. And all I had felt in that same second was an overwhelming sympathy for Stephanie. As I explained in Chapter One, I'm a mental medium, not a channeler. Channelers consent to letting deceased souls possess their bodies and display various behaviors through them. But I had not agreed to this. I had merely heard a voice within me say, "She needs a kiss." And I gave her one. So, without getting this back story from Greg's mother, I would never have understood the *real* reason for what I did.

I had read in other mediums' books years earlier that the spirits of the dead can "influence" the living to do various things in order to convey messages from the Other Side. We might be swayed by them, for instance, to offer our services or a gift to a grieving survivor of a tragic death. But I hadn't realized, until that moment in the Klaers' kitchen, just how quickly and automatically this could occur. The truth is it's so reflexive that you certainly don't need to be a medium for it to happen to you. In fact, the seemingly involuntary nature of this phenomenon, which I've come to call "temporary channeling," was again displayed that same day, by someone else.

I left the Klaers' home in early afternoon, along with my husband and the rest of the crowd of friends and relatives, who had gathered there to offer emotional support. And, as Greg's parents sat down to supper that evening with their surviving son, daughter, son-in-law, and two grandchildren, something surprising happened. What was a somber meal became unexpectedly lively and entertaining as their daughter's husband, Jason, began chattering at the table. Usually a man of few words, he suddenly started telling jokes and horsing around. Given the circumstances, this might have struck the family as inappropriate, if not for the fact that almost everything Jason was saying and doing was precisely what Greg would have said and done.

Oddly, Jason didn't seem aware his behavior had changed. Yet, every word and phrase he chose was like Greg's—a fact that led Rick and Stephanie to identify it as temporary channeling, once I shared the signs of visitation with them later that week.

The back story about this "visited" supper was that Greg would not have missed that family gathering for the world. His sister, brother-in-law, niece, and nephew had traveled by car all the way from Colorado to be with the rest of the Klaers family for Christmas. Greg adored his young niece and nephew, and he had relished the few holidays they were able to spend together through the years. So, his need to play the family clown was intense that evening. He was going to reach out to his loved ones and make them laugh, even though he had to commandeer someone else's body to do so.

Notice that in both of these cases of temporary channeling, Greg displayed benevolent behavior. This is what distinguishes temporary channeling from "possession." Possession, feared by humankind for millennia, is defined as being "possessed and dominated by evil spirits." So, the behavior displayed by a possessed individual is usually selfish and sinister. What's more, it's not normally temporary, but can go on indefinitely, unless a qualified exorcist intervenes. Our deceased loved ones, on the other hand, are respectful enough of our free will not to engage in lengthy channeling through us or to cause us to do anything we would find morally objectionable.

While the behavior Jason and I exhibited, as Greg channeled through us that day, was out of character for both of us, it wasn't harmful in any way. In fact, most temporary channeling is so subtle that the living don't even notice it, unless they've been taught to do so. The channelers themselves may become puzzled or embarrassed, wondering why they said or did this or that, but such feelings are generally shrugged off and forgotten.

Later that night, as the Klaers family was sitting in their living room, the overhead lights dimmed briefly, then returned to their usual brightness. There seemed to be no explanation for this, since there were no storms or high winds in the area and the wiring in the house was not prone to brown-outs or electrical problems.

There's no back story needed with this sign. It's a classic indication of visitation by the dead. Because they function at a speed that still confounds our conventional science, interfering with electrical systems appears to be one of the easiest ways for our deceased loved ones to say, "Hello. I'm here with you." It's so easy for the dead, in fact, that it certainly wouldn't be the last time Greg did it.

When I returned to the Klaers' home to do a full-fledged medium session a few days later, Stephanie requested a sign from her son that was meant for her alone. Greg told me to inform her that she should look for it in the kitchen. Less than 24 hours later, Greg chose to convey this sign through an electrical appliance that only his mom used: the coffeemaker.

The back story: Although Stephanie is an excellent cook, she had found less time for preparing meals through the years. Her children were grown and her work schedule more demanding. Thus her sons and husband sometimes teasingly remarked that the only time they saw her in the kitchen was when she was making coffee. That said, what better appliance for Greg to tamper with than his mom's coffeemaker in order to get her attention? He electrically manipulated it from the Other Side so that his mother was unable to turn it on. Yet, a moment later, his sister got it going with the usual press of the start button! This was a prankish sign to be sure, but it totally fit Greg's personality.

The Signs of Visitation

Clearly, Greg was not about to let death stand in his way where his family was concerned. He'd given the requested sign to his mom, and he now owed one to his father. So, as Rick Klaers sat typing part of his son's eulogy into his PC a couple days later, the sign appeared.

It was a speech no parent should ever have to write: a public goodbye tribute to a son who would probably have lived another sixty years, had his job not led him to be brutally stabbed to death. Rick had a couple paragraphs written when he got up from his computer to take a short break. When he returned, there was a sentence typed beneath what he had already written. Nevertheless, he was certain that no one in the house had come anywhere near his PC. While the sentence was out of character for Rick, it sounded very much like some of the Goth poetry Greg had written in the past. It was a morose reference to tragedy and death.

Rick later asked me, by phone, if it's possible for the dead to type messages into our PCs. I told him I've certainly heard accounts of it happening. It's not a common sign of visitation, nor is it apt to happen with the spirit of someone who did not use computers when he or she was alive. But Greg was young and PC savvy, so he was a good candidate for this form of afterlife communication. I'm not saying an observer will actually see the letter keys on a computer console typing out words at the selective pressures of invisible fingers. I've never heard or read of anyone witnessing that. Rather, given our deceased loved ones' abilities to manipulate almost anything electrical, the messages they want to send are probably generated from within the PC itself.

This was a remarkable sign of visitation. But the one I found most interesting from Greg Klaers was one that involved at least five people: relatives and friends, from three separate households. This sign came to our notice about a week after Greg's death, when a few of us, who were very close friends of Rick and Stephanie, met for dinner at a restaurant. During the meal, Greg's mom complained of not being able to sleep. Insomnia is not unusual after an event as traumatic as losing a family member to murder. What made it extraordinary was that Stephanie specified a time when she was inexplicably awakened each night: 3:00 a.m.

When I heard this I was taken aback, because it suddenly occurred to me that I, too, had been waking up at precisely that hour since Greg's death. But, after noticing the time on the alarm clock on the dresser in our bedroom, I would fall back to sleep and not remember it during my waking hours.

Even more amazing was the fact that both Rick Klaers and my husband chimed in at this point in our dinner conversation to report that they, too, had been waking up briefly at 3:00 a.m. each morning. Then, our mutual friend Dave said he was having the same 3:00 a.m. experiences!

In all my years of doing medium work, I had never heard of a sign affecting so many non-blood-related people. So, why was Greg disturbing all of us at this ungodly hour? What was the back story?

Greg's parents explained that this was when Greg returned home from his security-guard job each night. In fact, a couple weeks after Greg's death, Rick got up at 3:00 a.m., because he was sure he *heard* Greg coming upstairs to their bedroom!

This hour had become one of Greg's "signature" signs, his bona-fide way of saying to each one of us, "Hi. It's Greg. Don't forget about me." To this day, several years after his murder, Greg still wakes me, and his parents, at 3:00 a.m. whenever he wants a medium session with his family or when there's a significant occurrence in the legal hearings concerning his murder.

The final sign Greg gave in the week after he died is one you'll recognize, after reading Chapter One, as being a result of "clairalience." When I met with the Klaers family to give them a medium session several days after Greg's death, I showed them a

The Signs of Visitation

list of signs of visitation. This lengthy list, which I'll provide for you in this chapter, includes "unexplained smells" you might associate with your deceased loved one. And this sign prompted Greg's only brother Andy to tell me he had caught a whiff of Greg's male body spray, "Axe"® floating past him days after Greg died.

Notice that, of the seven signs Greg's family members reported receiving from him in the week following his death, this is the *only* one that entailed the use of a soul sense to perceive it. This illustrates that the majority of signs and messages our deceased loved ones send us don't require anything more than our five bodily senses to be recognized by us. You certainly don't need to be a medium or even a particularly gifted soul senser to pick up on most of the signs of spirit visitation.

They include:

- Interference with electrical or candle light.
- Mysteriously fallen or moved objects.
- The sound of footsteps in areas where your passed loved one usually walked.
- Inexplicable warm spots or indentations on your dead loved one's favorite furniture, cushions, or pillows.
- Unexplained tapping sounds.
- Inexplicable shadows cast on walls, floors, or ceilings.
- Being mysteriously woken at a significant hour of the night or early morning.
- Ringing doorbells or telephones with no apparent individual calling.
- Unexplained smells (such as the perfume, aftershave, or cigarette smoke of your deceased loved one. This can include any scent you would associate with him or her).

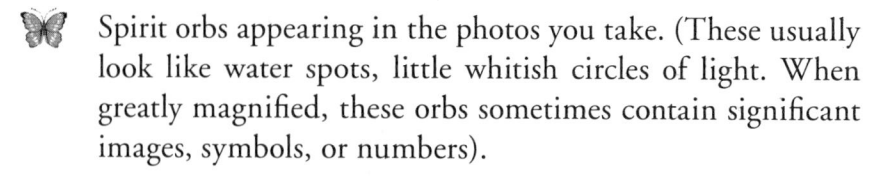

- Spirit orbs appearing in the photos you take. (These usually look like water spots, little whitish circles of light. When greatly magnified, these orbs sometimes contain significant images, symbols, or numbers).
- Interference with appliances.
- Interference with computers.
- Clocks or watches that stop or start at times that are significant (such as the hour of your loved one's death).
- Temporary channeling through living family members, friends, or pets. This means your deceased loved one's behavior, phrasing, or word choices will be briefly exhibited by a living individual.
- Night dreams with your passed relative or friend in them.
- Messages left on answering machines, cell phones, or other recording devices, usually in a voice you will recognize as your dead loved one's.
- Interference with your car's radio or electrical system.
- Music, which you associate with your passed loved one, playing more often or at significant times on your radio or TV.
- Miraculous gifts or healing. Spirits can silently persuade others to buy us gifts they want us to have, and they can bring Heavenly healing to us when we are sick or suffering.
- Rescue visitations—being physically saved from a fall or other dangerous situation.
- Out-of-body shifts during physically painful or frightening incidents.

The Signs of Visitation

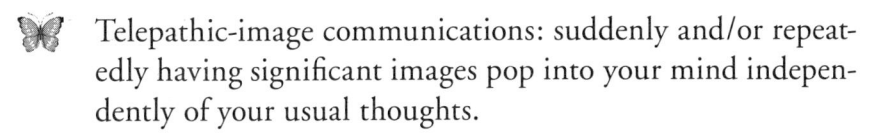

- Telepathic-image communications: suddenly and/or repeatedly having significant images pop into your mind independently of your usual thoughts.

- Unexplained drawings or writing in dust on objects or furnishings or in steam or other residue on walls or horizontal surfaces.

- The mysterious appearance of small objects, such as coins, buttons, leaves, or feathers in a place where they would not naturally be found. This is known as "apporting," which is defined as bringing forth objects from an unseen dimension.

- Pertinent messages conveyed through music or radio and TV broadcasts.

As with so many who've lost someone to death, none of Greg's relatives seemed certain they were being visited by his spirit, even though the signs of it were extensive. The living usually dismiss these signs as being either products of their imaginations or mere coincidences. But centuries of accounts of unexplained happenings soon after the death of a loved one indicate they are very real. So, when we shrug off these signs, we cast aside one of the greatest forms of love our deceased family and friends can extend to us. **It takes a lot of energy for spirits to give the living signs of their presence. If it didn't, they would do it more often.** Thus it's essential that we learn this very basic language of the dead. It's a precious gift from Heaven, as well as confirmation of the afterlife.

While our passed family members and friends bring through most of their signs of visitation within the first three months after their deaths, it has been my experience that you will continue to receive these signs for as long as you are attentive to them. I have many clients who report receiving these signs *years* after the deaths of their loved ones.

To get the most out of the signs of visitation, let's take a closer look at some of them.

Interference with electrical or candle light

Telling ghost stories around a campfire is an ancient tradition because the dead are attracted to the elements of life (fire, water, wind, and soil) and flame is particularly easy for them to manipulate in order to signal their presence. This is probably due to the fact that flame is pure energy: an oxidation of a combustible material releasing heat and light. The souls of our loved ones are more energy than substance, so they are in their own element when dealing with fire, and they can mold and influence it in remarkable ways. For example, a candle's flame may simply flicker in response to the presence of a spirit or that same soul may choose to extinguish the light altogether.

A final explanation of how the dead manipulate electrical lights will one day have to be offered by physicists. But what I see clairvoyantly when I ask the deceased about this is that they are somehow able to actually *touch* electrical current, as opposed to influencing it telepathically. This interferes with its flow and causes it to falter. Thus we see flickering or dimming lights when a passed soul wishes to communicate in this fashion. I've never heard of a case wherein electrical lights were shut off entirely. But this is possible as well. Being left in the dark, however, can be both frightening and annoying for the living, and that's probably why benevolent spirits avoid doing it.

The most informative case I've heard about electrical interference occurred in 2003, when one of my clients, a woman named Linda, asked to speak through me to her deceased father. I told Linda that her dad was telling me he had recently been with her when she had attended a recital of some kind. She confirmed that she had been at her niece's dance recital a week earlier.

"But your father says something went wrong with the lighting."

"Yes. That's right. The stage lights suddenly became so bright that no one could videotape or photograph the dancers without a blinding glare interfering."

"Your dad says he was watching your niece (his granddaughter) from overhead as she danced in the recital. He says she was wearing a pink costume."

"Yes, she was."

"He's apologizing."

"For what?" Linda asked, sounding mystified.

"For accidentally getting caught up in the spotlights. He says *he* caused them to glow too brightly."

Linda was silent for a few seconds. I assumed she was finding this explanation as incredible as I was. To my surprise, she replied, "That makes total sense to me."

"It does?"

"Yes. He was an electrician in life. And he was almost electrocuted once. It wasn't enough to kill him. But it left him unable to use his right hand for small motor skills, like writing. Anyway, the electrical fields in his body were never the same after that. So, it makes sense that he could interfere with the stage lights."

What a back story!

Inexplicable warm spots or indentations on furniture, cushions, or pillows

So many of my clients have mentioned that they've felt warm spots and indentations on their deceased loved one's bed or favorite chair, that I now advise the living to respect the "space" of the deceased for several weeks or months after his or her passing. If your family member or pet preferred to sit or lie on a certain chair or cushion, it's safe to assume he or she will continue to do so whenever visiting you. So it's best to leave it unoccupied as much as possible.

If your spouse is the one who has passed away, some grief counselors will advise you to sleep on his or her usual side of the bed or sit in his or her chair at the kitchen or dining-room table. This is sound advice. It helps relieve loneliness. But, if you always follow this counsel, you may miss out on the wondrous experience of physically feeling your loved one's presence via the indentation and/or warmth their spirit bodies sometimes leave on furniture, cushions, and pillows.

I remember a medium session during which a passed husband told his wife how pleased he was to have had a seat next to her on a commercial flight home from a recent European vacation she'd taken. "That's right," she exclaimed, surprised that I knew about this occurrence before she had mentioned it to me. "The flights are packed with passengers these days. But, for some reason, I had an empty seat next to me on the trip back to New York."

Had she known to touch the empty seat cushion next to her, she probably would have felt evidence that it had, indeed, been occupied—by her lifelong companion and travel mate. While the dead are not subject to the same physical discomforts as the living, they don't seem fond of "standing-room-only" situations, especially prolonged ones. That's why it's best to leave a seat open for them whenever possible.

While we're on the subject of furniture, it's not unusual for widows or widowers to tell me they're convinced their deceased spouses still share their beds at night. What's more, my communications with their passed husbands and wives confirm that they do, in fact, take time out from their activities in Heaven to lie in their earthly beds at night. They claim this is not only to keep their spouses company, but also to guard them from any harm as they sleep. Our dead loved ones tend to be very protective of us.

I don't recall any cases in which my clients have reported actually seeing their spouses' souls lying next to them. Instead, they physically feel them in the bed or they reflexively use their clairsentience (the soul sense which allows them to feel sensations instilled by a visiting spirit) in order to confirm they are there.

Because I know you're probably wondering, I'll answer your next logical question now: Yes, it is possible for the living to have sex with a disembodied spirit. Soul mates remain soul mates, even if one of them is out of body and the other is not. This kind of coupling is much like what you might experience in an erotic dream. It involves a combination of physical sensations, clairsentience, and access through the base chakra.

Ringing Doorbells or Telephones With No Apparent Individual Calling

Nothing gets the attention of the living like a ringing phone or doorbell. So, don't be surprised if this is one of the ways your deceased loved one tells you, "I'm here. Pay attention to me."

In a world filled with automated telemarketing systems dialing two lines at once and hanging up on the party who answers second, it can be difficult to tell if the hang-up calls you receive after the death of a loved one are from that soul or from a telemarketer. Phone solicitations generally end by nine o'clock p.m., however, and don't resume until about that hour in the morning, so any hang-up calls you receive between those hours may be significant.

It's also interesting to note that there are far more reports of deceased loved ones leaving messages on telephone answering machines and voice-mail systems, than of them actually speaking to the living party on the other end of the phone. This is probably because the dead speak so quickly that we are much more likely to capture their voices on audiotape, than to hear them with our ears.

As for the deceased ringing our doorbells, this sign is much harder to misread than a hang-up call. It happened to me one evening, as my husband and I were preparing to go to a wedding. My husband was showering and I was already dressed and waiting for him, when someone rang our doorbell. I was standing near our entryway and answered it within seconds, but no one was there. I hurried outside, looked up and down the street, but still didn't see anyone.

It wasn't until we were at the wedding reception that evening and the bride and groom were making toasts that I realized who my invisible caller had been. When my friend, the bride, mentioned how sorry she was that her only sibling, a brother who had died in a car accident years before, could not be there on this joyous occasion, I silently acknowledged how mistaken she was in assuming that her brother was not present.

I told the newlyweds about it later. But I also realized it wouldn't have done any good for the bride's brother to ring *her* doorbell, because she is far too skeptical about such afterlife communications to have recognized it as a sign of visitation. He knew, however, that he could count on me to correctly interpret it and pass the message on to her.

I had never encountered an invisible doorbell ringer before then, nor have I since. But some of my clients have told me that spirit doorbell ringing, like all other signs of visitation that involve electrical devices, can become quite a nuisance. In some cases, the spirit's energy is so powerful that the doorbell will keep ringing off and on, until it finally has to be disconnected or replaced. One of these days, an electrician will have to team up with a quantum physicist to explain to us laymen exactly how a spirit can cause a doorbell to malfunction in this manner. One thing I can tell you with relative certainty, however, is that this is an accidental development, since it is rarely our deceased loved ones' intent to break our belongings or make relentless pests of themselves.

Spirit Orbs in Your Photos

Because seeing is believing for most of us, there seems to be no more compelling sign of visitation than finding spirit orbs in the photos we take after the deaths of loved ones. These small, whitish circles of unexplained light in camera still shots can lead to the living mistakenly believing the photos are defective and throwing them away! On the contrary, these can be some of the dearest treasures our dead can extend to us. What's more, you don't need expensive photographic equipment or well-developed soul senses to capture them.

I've seen hundreds of photos with spirit orbs in them, because my clients often email them to me. Mediums can usually predict when orbs will appear in photos, so my customers like to show me the evidence that my predictions have come true. To date, though, I've seen no more remarkable orbs than those Greg Klaers offered his family a couple days after he was murdered. I had advised Greg's parents to snap pictures on Christmas Eve, because I felt certain Greg would put spirit orbs in them. And, indeed, he did.

Manifesting orbs is quite an achievement for the dead, but Greg took the process several steps further. When his parents emailed me the photos of their December 24th family gathering, I magnified all of the spirit orbs in them. The majority of them just looked like spots with nothing visible in their centers. But two of them, when enlarged, proved to be absolutely astounding.

The first was a grayish orb over the Klaers' fireplace, which, when magnified several times, contained numbers and one lowercase letter written in perfect handwriting. It looked as if it had been written by a fingertip on a frost-covered window. The message read: 4 24s

"Four twenty fours?" I repeated to Stephanie and Rick, when they came to my home to look at the magnifications on my computer. "What does that mean to you?"

"Well, Greg was twenty-four years old when he died," Stephanie replied. "And the photos were taken on the twenty-fourth of December."

That accounted for two of the four twenty fours. But now, years later, we're still waiting for clarification about the other two.

Fortunately, Greg's second orb message needed no explanation. It was located in another photo, resting upon the arm of Greg's nephew Zach. Even without magnification, I could tell this orb was extraordinary. Instead of reflecting the flesh tone of Zach's arm or the bright hue of his solid blue shirt, it looked like it contained mysterious splashes of brown and black. And, as I zoomed in on it with my computer, I was absolutely amazed to see a small, furry, full-colored dog!

Critics of spirit-orb photography argue that people often imagine they see faces in them because humans are programmed from birth to focus upon the faces of their parents and other caregivers. But I didn't just see a dog's face in this orb; I saw the full-length body of a terrier, complete with legs, ears, and a tail! Although the dog was headed towards the right in the photo, its face was turned back towards me, as though whoever had taken this Heaven-sent picture had called its name upon snapping it. Also, the fact that the image was captured in full color is phenomenal, since the vast majority of orb images are black and white.

When I showed this orb to Rick and Stephanie, they didn't hesitate in identifying the canine. Though they had owned several dogs through the years, they recognized this one as being Katie, the elderly Yorkshire terrier who had died on the same day Greg had. The family believed that the timing of Katie's death by an apparent heart attack was no accident. She had been ailing for a while and they were convinced that Greg, an animal lover, had decided to take her to Heaven with him. However, he clearly wanted his parents to have this orb "photo" of her as she looked

The Signs of Visitation

in her youth. It seemed to be his way of saying, "Katie's with me now. Don't worry. And she's young and healthy again." What more poignant Christmas gift could he have given his family? And how blessed they were not to have missed out on it.

Be sure you don't pass over this miraculous gift from the afterlife. Make a note on your calendar to take photos on such special occasions as your deceased loved one's birthday, wedding anniversaries, and those holidays when you feel his or her spirit will be joining you. Most computer photo software programs feature easy-to-use zoom-in controls, once you open a given picture. They're often depicted as a magnifying glass and plus and minus symbols for making an image within your photo larger or smaller. So you can magnify any orbs you find and discover the images or messages that may be hidden within them. Even if you find your orbs are empty, you should take comfort in these visible signs from the Other Side, which tell us our passed loved ones are close at hand and still a part of our earthly lives.

Temporary Channeling through Pets

Later in this book, I'll go into greater detail about temporary channeling by deceased loved ones through the living people around us. For now though, I'd like to advise you to be aware of and appreciate the behavior of family pets after you've lost a family member, friend, or another pet to death. The dead crave physical contact with those they've left behind on earth. But, because their souls or astral bodies can't always demonstrate physical affection to the living, they usually find it easiest to influence the animals in our lives to express that physicality for them.

So be observant when your pets begin to act more affectionately than usual after a death. Cats, dogs, birds, guinea pigs, and just about every other kind of domesticated animal have been known to give and need extra cuddles and hugs at such a sorrowful time. Temporarily, they *are* your lost loved one coming back to exchange physical touch with you and say, "I'm here with you. And my love for you will never die."

The Klaers Continue to Receive and Recognize the Signs of Visitation

For the Klaers, like most families, the language of the afterlife is one that needs to be learned and memorized. When I do medium sessions with them now, I can tell they have become conversant in this language, and they have continued to receive messages from Greg's soul since his death.

Their pets have shown signs of temporary channeling. "Twinkie", Greg's elderly cat, became more affectionate than usual after Greg died. She also began waking Greg's parents at the significant 3:00 a.m. hour. She would leap up on their bedroom dresser and knock toiletries onto the floor, making enough noise to tell them when Greg wanted another medium session with them.

Their spirit-orb photography continued as well. Because Greg had always wanted to take a trip to Las Vegas, his parents traveled there for him after his death. While there, they went to a Karaoke bar, since singing Karaoke-style was one of Greg's earthly pastimes. I predicted that, when they did this, they would hear two songs they could identify at Greg's favorites. Not only did they hear those two tunes, but spirit orbs appeared solely in the photos they snapped when those two songs were being sung—even though they took photos of many Karaoke performers that evening.

When it came time to clean out Greg's bedroom, Stephanie and Rick again had their camera ready and Greg came through for them once more. Not only were there spirit orbs in their pictures of his room, but Greg sent them a collection of images they recognized, all contained within one large orb! Stephanie and Rick showed me this huge sphere on their computer. Moving clockwise around the outer edge of it, we could see first the face of an elderly man, whom the Klaers believed might be Rick's deceased father.

The Signs of Visitation

Then there was the image of an infant, whom Stephanie felt was that of a newborn who had recently died in her family. And there was an image of Greg holding their dead dog, Katie, which bore an amazing resemblance to a photo they'd taken of him and the terrier long before they had both died.

Stephanie seems less able to perceive signs of visitation than others in the family. So, she has been working on becoming more right-brained through creative activities. This must be working, because she recently told me she felt a warm spot and indentation at the foot of her bed. This confirmed for her that Greg had come to watch over her, because she was sick with the flu at that time.

The Klaers have received so many signs of visitation since Greg died that I cannot hope to remember or list them all here. But, just after the sentencing hearing for the man who murdered Greg, Rick Klaers told TV reporters that he still felt his son with him "all the time."

Soul-Sensing Summary

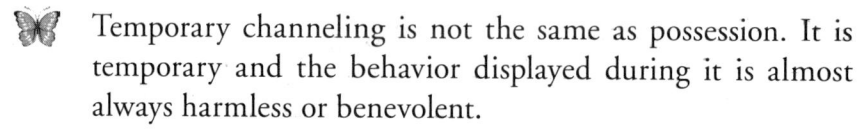

- You cannot fully decipher signs of visitation without knowing the back stories on them.

- Temporary channeling is not the same as possession. It is temporary and the behavior displayed during it is almost always harmless or benevolent.

- Many signs of visitation by the dead do not require the use of soul senses to be recognized.

- It takes a lot of energy on the part of the dead to show signs of visitation to the living. If it didn't, they would do it more often.

- Don't miss out on spirit orbs from your deceased loved ones and pets. Make a note on your calendar to take photographs on significant dates and holidays. Photos that can be downloaded to your computer will allow you to study any images or messages contained within the orbs.

Chapter 3

Why Soul Sensing Works

Approximately one billion years ago something was born on the earth that would change life forever: *death*. That's right. As mysterious, impenetrable, and inevitable as death seems to us now, it's actually a relatively new occurrence on our planet, since the earth is estimated to be four billion years old.

For 75% of the earth's history, there was no death—which is defined in most dictionaries as the discarding of a corpse. The reason for this is that early life on this planet was of the single-cell variety. This life reproduced itself by splitting in half. So, where there was one amoeba, there were eventually two, then three, then four. And the original parent of these did not die of natural causes, but, rather became many single cells over time.

As life evolved into more complex forms, however, asexual reproduction (just splitting in half) became impossible for them. When that happened, both sexual reproduction and death were born. Thus we know that the state we call "death" is linked to sexual reproduction. It binds us to matter, to the earth, and to physical mortality.

This may be why those of us who are not capable of procreation *due to age or life stage* (children and postmenopausal women) are more likely to sense the presence of deceased loved ones than the rest of the population. It's been documented many times, for instance, that kids report seeing the spirits of the dead far more often than adults do.

Sex and Death

Death is the price we pay for sex; and it sure seems like a very high price for us, given that our asexual fellow earth dwellers enjoy what can be defined as eternal life. How is it possible for amoebas to be more deserving of immortality than we humans are? The answer is they're not. They're just such a simple life form that they're easier to maintain on the physical plane indefinitely. They are only a step outside the spiritual realm and just one step into the physical dimension of life, which has all sorts of innate limitations to it. Life in the physical world, while spectacularly tangible, is definitely limited in its duration for us sexual beings. The very tangibility of the physical world is what separates us from the realm of immortality.

It can be argued that we humans do enjoy a form of physical immortality through reproduction, in that some of our genes are passed on to the next generation. Unlike single-celled creatures, however, humans are each unique. Even identical twins differ from one another, both physically and in personality. In short, you are the only genetic version of yourself there will ever be. If you have children, you have or will pass on only a portion of your physical self to them; and that portion will get smaller and smaller with each generation born after you. What you long for is the ultimate survival of the "you" reflected in your mirror. Yet, your reflection is constantly changing and aging. For instance, displayed in my living room are some framed photos taken of my nephews and nieces when they were in grade school. Those shy, soft-spoken little people no longer exist, however. Nor have they died. They've simply aged so much that these early images of them would not help you recognize who they are today. They, like all of us, have changed considerably through the years.

The eternal essence of humans is probably not very physical in nature. Our personalities, our beliefs, our wisdom, our memories, our passions, our likes and dislikes are all less manifest than our physical bodies. These personality traits may also change with the passing years, but they seem somehow "soul" deep. They are more resilient and less vulnerable to the passage of time, as well as to those outside elements which age and damage the cells of our physical bodies.

We're Actually Only Energy

Now, having established how solid, if changeable, our physical bodies are when compared to our little amoeba friends, it's time to consider one of the other great ironies of our physical life on the earth: we're not all that solid, after all. We humans, like almost everything else that surrounds us in this world, are composed of atoms. They make us appear to be substantive, but an atom actually consists mainly of space: a positively charged nucleus that exerts an electrical attraction on one or more electrons in orbit around it. This means that every creature on earth is made up of little more than very fast-moving energy.

When I was in high school, my biology teacher explained all of this in a way that even I, a completely right-brained, non-science-oriented, creative type could understand. "Imagine," he said to my 10th-grade class, "that you are trying to step into one of the doors of this school building, but someone is running around the outside of this same building so fast that, every time you try to enter it, you bump into that person and it feels like you're hitting a brick wall. That's how fast an electron circles a nucleus. It's moving so quickly that you don't see it, but it's speeding around so often that it seems to be constantly in your way, as if it were a solid wall."

Subatomic Particles

So, here we are: we multi-cellular, sexual beings who seem solid, but who are composed mainly of space and very fast-moving energy. And, because eternal life was the original state on our planet and we have an intrinsic desire for immortality, we can't help but wonder what part of us survives after death. What portion of us constitutes the elusive "soul" which our ancestors have believed in for eons? Some physicists have concluded that the answer to this is subatomic particles. These particles are even smaller than atoms. They're so minute and speedy, in fact, that scientists must define them by their behavior, because they cannot be observed with our physical senses.

Some subatomic particles, for example, can be in two places at once. They can move through solid surfaces, such as walls and closed doors. They can also disappear, then reappear, almost instantly, in another location. According to world-famous physicist, Michio Kaku, scientists studying these behaviors in Victorian England asked themselves, "What have we seen or heard about that can do all of these things?" Their answer was *"ghosts!"*

Physicists like Kaku take this study further, into theories of higher dimensions and parallel universes. But, for the purpose of explaining why soul sensing works, I'll stick with the topic of the subatomic levels of human beings. My focus in this chapter is not on where we go when we die, but what form we take when we leave our dead bodies behind us. Learning more about our souls will help us better understand how to communicate with this level of ourselves, as well as how to receive messages from the souls of others.

Some scientists, such as William G. Roll, Ph.D., already have what seem to be some well-documented indications that the subatomic soul leaves the body at the time of physical death. They have noted that our bodies lose a variable number of grams of weight when we die, after accounting for the loss of fluids and air. Spirit photography indicates that the soul, or some version of it, can be captured on camera film and digital imaging. Spirit voices have been recorded thousands of times on audio tape. And, in countless reports of hauntings, unexplained cold spots develop, electrical lights flicker and dim, batteries go dead, and cameras or recording devices malfunction, as disembodied souls leech power from these systems in order to do the difficult work of communicating with the living, as well as re-manifesting themselves on the physical plane. I should also note here that the extensive spirit-orb studies of Miceal Ledwith and physicist Klaus Heinemann, Ph.D. led to these conclusions: spirit orbs are certainly not beings of the space-time world. And the light which these orbs emit is not a product of our physical plane.

Beings of Light

In my studies of the nature of the soul, the word "light" appeared time and again in scientific writings. The standard definition of light is "electromagnetic radiation." An electron, in turn, is a "fundamental constituent of matter, negatively charged and existing independently or as a component *outside* the nucleus of an atom."

In the 1970s, theoretical biologist Fritz-Albert Popp began experimenting with light (electromagnetic radiation) as a possible cure for cancer. During these experiments, he discovered there is light within the human body which is responsible for photo repair of cells. Popp went on to trace the source of this light and he learned that one of the key sites of it was DNA. He had happened upon one of the most miraculous processes in biology: the way in which a single cell ultimately grows into an entire human body. It is a function directed by light. And so it seems that we are connected with that first, eternal single-celled creature by this divine spark. Some physicists' research seems to indicate this light will continue to hold our cells together for the rest of our lives, because, once this electromagnetic force leaves the body at the time of death, the corpse begins to decay.

Scientific research points to the likelihood that the light emitted by all living creatures is not merely the result of body heat. Nor is it simply fluorescence (a product of radiation due to an external source). Rather, our body light is generated from deep within us. As Lynn McTaggart pointed out in her book, *The Field: The Quest for the Secret Force of the Universe,* this light imprint continues to be present, even after the physical limb or matter which emitted it has been removed—as in the case of an amputation of a limb. The phenomenon of the ghost limb indicates that every part of our physical bodies is, apparently, permanently impressed upon what McTaggart refers to as "the Zero Point Field."

Knowing this about the subatomic nature of the soul helps us make more sense of those accounts we've all heard of ghost sightings. For millennia, reports of ghosts have occurred in every country on earth, yet the behaviors described are all amazingly similar:

"One second, a translucent human form appeared, then it vanished." (As some subatomic particles can)

"This form was visible even in total darkness." (Emitting self-generated light)

"The form seemed to glide, rather than walk. Then it floated, and even flew, like an angel." (Not as bound by gravity as heavier, more physical matter is)

"The form moved right through a wall or closed door." (As some subatomic particles can)

"A dying relative was in one place, yet his or her spirit appeared to another family member or friend somewhere else at exactly the same time." (In two places at once, like some subatomic particles can be).

This, apparently, is the nature of the soul. And, as with scientists studying subatomic matter, what we're learning about it comes mainly from observing its behavior. The soul seems capable of doing so much our physical bodies cannot. It defies the laws of gravity, time, and space; yet it faces great limitations on the huge and heavy physical plane.

Let's again consider the signs of visitation listed in Chapter 2. Of the over two dozen I named there, none of them involves moving heavy objects. Rather, they are activities that are characteristic of very lightweight subatomic matter, such as manipulating electrical systems, influencing the thoughts and actions of the living, writing messages in dust or steam, and using fire, water, lights, and shadows as means of communication. These are the only things our deceased loved ones can do in their subatomic forms to get our attention on the physical plane. So, it's up to us, the living, to learn to read between the lines and develop our soul senses as fully as possible, if we wish to converse with them.

Our Subatomic Selves

Our soul senses are able to tap into the world of the dead, because they, like disembodied souls, function on the subatomic level. Unlike our physical senses, soul senses are not bound by the usual laws of gravity, time, or space. This is why some of the messages we receive from them foretell future events. Ask any professional medium and he or she will tell you that "telling time" is one of the toughest parts of mediumship. Our soul senses only know that a given event takes place—whether that is in a client's past, present, or future is far less clear. Subatomic matter, like our non-temporal right brains, has very little sense of linear time.

In addition, our soul senses do not rely on physical stimulation in order to gather information. While our brains can only process about 2,000 of the 400 billion pieces of information our physical senses take in per second, our soul senses can gather and process more. And, ultimately, it is not what our senses perceive, but what our brains acknowledge that truly shapes our reality.

Even more amazing is the fact that matter itself is affected by our perception of it. When we are *not* looking at an object, for example, its atoms form a wave. But, when we *are* looking at that same object, our focus causes its atoms to coalesce into something substantial. In other words, our perception of them actually makes them more solid! Thus we, as observers, play an inextricable role in the process of soul sensing.

If you've ever felt you were being watched, but you could not put your finger on who was watching you or from where, you've experienced this form of clairsentience firsthand. The very act of that party's observation sent signals to your atoms to become more concentrated. The subatomic activity caused by this told your brain, "I'm being watched. I'm not alone here."

Ghost hunters, for example, often get the "sense" of a presence in the settings they're investigating, but they can't document what they're feeling until they employ electronic equipment and their readings confirm their hunches. This is the nature of the subatomic world all around us, as well as our own subatomic abilities to perceive it. These perceptions are so minute and fleeting that we have to work at making them register in our brains. We must learn to pay attention to them and not just write them off as being products of our imaginations or mere coincidences.

Our seven soul senses are just as legitimate as our five physical ones. Once we accept and become attuned to this subatomic level of ourselves, we open the door to those in the afterlife, as well as the messages they want to share with us. As with radio waves, which are also invisible, yet very real, it's all just a matter of learning to tune into the right frequencies.

Inkling. Hunch. Shiver. Tingle. Sneaking suspicion. Gut feeling. Impression. Intuition. Sixth sense. Until now, all of these words have been our vague ways of saying one thing: "The subatomic level of yourself is receiving a message." And, most often, this message is coming from someone else's subatomic level, be they dead or alive.

Pinpointing Your Perceptions

In coming chapters, I'll teach you ways in which to become more aware of these messages and determine who is sending them. You'll also learn how to decipher and respond to them. For now, however, I urge you to pay attention to any internal perceptions you might experience. Start a soul-sensing journal and make note of what sensations you feel and *where* in your body you feel them. Odds are your subatomic self will be most stimulated in the areas where physicist Klaus Heinemann, Ph.D. discovered we function at the highest electromagnetic gauge symmetry levels: our seven chakras. These include the crown of your head, the brow area of your forehead, your throat, neck and shoulders, your solar plexus, your pelvic region and the base of your spine.

Include with these journal notes any significant events that are happening around the time you receive this subatomic stimulation, such a death or birth in your family or the anniversaries of any of these. As you begin to consciously connect your inner essence with the occurrences in the world around you, the subatomic feelings you experience and the messages you receive because of them will start to make more sense to you.

Soul-Sensing Summary

- Sexual reproduction binds us to matter, to the earth and to physical mortality.

- Our physical bodies are composed of atoms. They make us appear to be solid, but an atom consists mainly of space. So our bodies are made up of little more than very fast-moving energy.

- The eternal essence of us (our souls) appears to be composed of subatomic particles. These particles are so minute and speedy that they must be defined by their behavior, rather than our ability to observe them with our physical senses.

- Some subatomic particles can be in two places at once. They can move through solid surfaces, such as walls and closed doors. They can disappear, then reappear, almost instantly, in another location. This same behavior is often reported in ghost sightings.

- All matter is affected by our perception of it. When directly perceived, an object's atoms become more solid.

- Our soul senses are able to tap into the world of the dead, because they, like disembodied souls, function on the subatomic level.

- To find more in-depth explanations of the nature of subatomic matter and the effects of our perception upon it, I recommend you read the following: *The Orb Project* by Miceal Ledwith, D.D., LL.D. & Klaus Heinemann, Ph.D., *The Holographic Universe* by Michael Talbot, The Field by Lynne McTaggart, *Is There an Afterlife?: A Comprehensive Overview of the Evidence* by David Fontana; and watch "Your Immortal Brain" by Dr. Joe Dispenza.

Chapter 4

The Real Barriers

Those I've Helped Master Their Doubts and Fears

If you have doubts, not only about your ability to use soul senses to bring through messages from deceased loved ones, but *anyone's* ability to do so, I highly recommend two steps to you. The first is that you go back to Chapter 3 of this book and read or re-read it, so that you understand the science behind the process of soul sensing.

The second is that you make an appointment with a reputable medium, one who asks for little or no identifying information about your deceased loved one before your afterlife-communication session. Having a private appointment with a gifted medium should eliminate the doubts you might have felt at watching medium work being done in large groups, on TV shows, or hearing it on the radio. Although I've never heard of "plants" being placed in such audiences, a personal session insures that the medium who's reading for you has no foreknowledge of the passed party you wish to reach and that he or she is actually using soul senses to bring information and messages to you from the Other Side.

Avoid mediums who ask for a photograph of the deceased party you wish to contact. Some of them do! And by so doing, they've virtually eliminated the opportunity to prove to you they're immediately connecting with your loved one by bringing through descriptive information about that person or pet. Specifics like eye color, hair color and length, as well as other physical characteristics of your departed are part and parcel of what a genuine medium delivers. The medium may also offer other details which you can verify, such as your dead loved one's occupation, cause of death, personality traits, etc. Let the medium choose which specifics to bring through to you, as long as these specifics convince you you're being put in contact with the spirit you seek. Having such a one-on-one opportunity to communicate with the afterlife through a professional medium is crucial to many beginning soul sensors. It helps them begin to believe in their own mediumistic abilities.

While you should carry a certain amount of "show-me" attitude into any session with a medium, be sure to keep an open mind about afterlife communications. Just because a particular medium does not turn out to be a good match for you personally, does not mean all mediums are ineffective or that talking to the deceased is impossible.

Getting Out of Your Own Way

I assume, since you're reading this book, you have no hidden agenda to sabotage the soul-sensing process, but assumptions can sometimes get one into trouble. A case in point was a session I did (or, more precisely *tried* to do) for a new client not long ago. This lady, whom I'll call Natalie, said she had heard me doing medium work for callers on a radio show. So, I *assumed* she had been impressed with my accuracy on the air and that was why she had called me for an appointment. She wanted an in-person, rather than phone session, so I arranged it for her. Then she called shortly before the scheduled time and cancelled without explanation. A few weeks later, she phoned me, again wanting to set up an in-person session, and I agreed to it.

The Real Barriers

I do all of my in-person appointments in a local metaphysical establishment, so I again arranged it for her. But she said she was not happy with that location and that she wanted to meet me at a nearby restaurant instead. I explained to her that such a setting would be too disruptive and noisy for me to do quality medium work for her there. This was met by silence on the other end of the phone, as if it had never even occurred to her that it was possible for mediumistic abilities to be disrupted. Then she grudgingly agreed to my usual location. By this time, I knew she was a difficult sort, but I hadn't yet sensed how difficult. She was obviously controlling, but she seemed to want to talk to one of her deceased pets so desperately that she could only acquiesce to my need for a quiet place in which to work.

Upon meeting her, I was struck by how cold and unlikeable she seemed. This is highly unusual for me, since I find nine-tenths of my clients a joy to serve. After introducing herself to me and vice versa, she sat down at my reading table and her first question bowled me over. "Is this for real?" she asked, crinkling the bridge of her nose at me. "I mean, really, can you honestly talk to my dead cat?"

I resisted the temptation to ask her what on earth she was doing meeting with me, if she honestly didn't think I could. I must admit that, on a gut level, I was also struck by how rude these questions were. I am, after all, one of the only mediums I know who offers a money-back guarantee of contact with the deceased parties my clients wish to reach. I suppose it should go without saying that this is not the sort of offer charlatans make. But this simple truth did not seem evident to Natalie. Being a professional, however, I chose not to react defensively to her. I figured, once I began bringing through specifics about her deceased cat, she would realize I was, indeed, the real deal.

I admit that reading for her was not easy. Her negative energy was fighting me and what pieces of identifying information I could bring through for her about her passed pet were interspersed with her grumblings about how she was on the outs with her husband, her niece, and her in-laws. I couldn't help but feel that I was somehow slated to be next on her on-the-outs-with list.

I proceeded to correctly tell her the color of her dead pet, some of the cat's personality traits, and even precisely where in her house she kept a framed photo of this feline. Even though she confirmed that all of this identifying information was correct, she, to my utter amazement, again leaned towards me and asked, "Is this for real?"

By that point, I was tempted to say something utterly preposterous to her, such as, "No. You see, even though I don't know your address or even your last name, I've been spying on you for several months. Even before your cat passed away, I was surreptitiously learning everything I could about her. So that, when you finally called me for an appointment, I'd be armed with all this information in order to trick you out of a one-hour session fee."

Instead, realizing she was never going to be satisfied that *anyone* possessed soul-sensing or medium ability, I told her I was not the right reader for her and that she should find a more suitable one. With that, I gathered up my purse and strode out of the store, having not received a penny for my time or effort on that sub-zero morning. All I had received was a heaping helping of unwarranted disrespect.

I had never walked out on a client before then, and I hope never to have to again. Nevertheless, the valuable moral of this true tale is: if you have some secret desire to reject all evidence of afterlife communications, you are not a good candidate for them. You will not only hamper your own efforts at them, but probably those of any medium you hire. If you should meet with ongoing difficulties when it comes to soul sensing, dig deeply into your belief systems. If some part of you believes it's impossible, it probably will be. I could not help Natalie, because even firsthand evidence of mediumship did not convince her that this ability exists. I have, however, convinced thousands of others that it does.

Seeing With Your Eyes Closed

Once you've finished confronting any negativity which you're consciously or unconsciously bringing into your soul-sensing efforts, ask yourself this: How, with my eyes closed, do I see the colors, images, and activities in my dreams at night? You might argue that dreams are simply images stored in the memory cells of your mind. The fact is, however, many dreams are not composed of memories, but are themselves new experiences. So, what visual organ is watching what happens in your dreams and reporting it to your brain as you sleep?

The answer is your "mind's eye," clairvoyance, the most-often-used of the seven soul senses. Since you employ it almost every night, it is remarkably strong. This means you can eventually learn to apply it while you're awake.

I also encourage you to begin keeping track of the other soul senses you use when dreaming. Upon waking each morning, take a minute to ask yourself what you remember about last night's dreams. Note not only what you saw in them, but what you may have felt (clairsentience), heard (clairaudience), smelled (clairalience), or tasted (clairgustance). This easy exercise will help you get in touch with your soul senses during your waking hours.

It's also important to understand that soul sensing develops more slowly in some people than in others. It takes practice and perseverance, and some of the methods offered in this book will work better for you than others will. I, therefore, urge you to try each of them and be patient with yourself and the passed loved one(s) with whom you're trying to communicate.

Have a Little Faith

I've noticed that those who have the most difficulty with soul sensing are not only doubters, but they have little or no faith in others. They are, like my disgruntled would-be client Natalie, obsessed with maintaining control. Giving yourself over to Heaven, in order to communicate with your loved ones who are there, means relinquishing control of the process to some extent. As with meditation, there's a good measure of "letting go and letting God" involved. Have some faith in the spirits of your deceased loved ones and, eventually, they will come through for you.

Years ago, long before I had written this book with all of its tips on soul sensing, a coworker of mine named Michael complained that, even though other members of his family had received messages and visits from his deceased father, Michael hadn't heard or seen a thing from him. He told me he felt hurt and jealous that his dad had communicated with others, but not him. Michael was both very competitive and controlling. Yet, it wasn't until he was seemingly helpless that his father came to him.

Michael had just received his small-plane pilot's license. He was flying home one evening, after a short trip to the family's cabin, when the plane's engine started cutting out. He was frantic, utterly out of control, when, all of a sudden, he heard his dad's voice in his head. His father had been a fighter pilot during WWII, and the advice he gave his son in those fateful moments enabled Michael to land the sputtering plane in a nearby open field and walk away from what mechanics later told him should have been a fiery crash.

Another very controlling, left-brain friend of mine, whom I'll call Susan, did not hear a peep from her deceased daughter, even though others in her family received visits from the girl's spirit. Then, one day, Susan developed a nasty case of food poisoning. She became very weak and bedridden, and only then did her daughter's soul appear to her. Susan's illness had made her lose a measure of control over her life that day, but she had gained something she would always treasure: another chance to visit with her dead daughter.

I should note here that physical illness can also block one's soul-sensing abilities. Many professional mediums, including me, cannot bring through afterlife messages consistently when they are sick. On the other hand, terminal illness often causes those in hospice care to report seeing and communicating with their deceased loved ones before they themselves die. With all of this said, however, it obviously was not Susan's illness that caused her to suddenly be able to commune with her dead daughter. It was the fact that her virus lowered her emotional and psychological defenses enough to allow her daughter's soul to make its presence known to her. Even if just for one day, infirmity made Susan less controlling.

Assessing Control Issues

It can be difficult to determine if you have a controlling personality, since many of the people in your life may be uncomfortable with telling you that you do. I've found, however, that, if you answer the following questions, you'll get a sense of whether or not control issues will block your soul-sensing abilities.

1. Do you usually insist on driving when you go places with family or friends?
2. Do you require the final say about which restaurant or movie you go to with others?
3. Is it difficult for you to trust your coworkers, subordinates, or employees to perform their tasks at work?
4. Do changes in your environment or procedures make you very uncomfortable?

5. Are you unwilling to try new foods or new vacation destinations?

6. Do you become deeply or lingeringly unhappy when you don't win at board games, cards, or sports you play with your friends or relatives?

Almost everyone feels a bit uneasy about some of the situations I've just listed. Nevertheless, if you answered "yes" to three or more of these questions, it may be time to try loosening up a little. If you *always* have to be in the driver's seat, always have to win at games, and always have to control the experiences you have with others in order to feel safe and content, your soul senses will probably elude you.

Opening Up to Heaven

Try putting more trust in others and in the workings of the universe, and you will be much more likely to succeed with afterlife communications. After all, soul sensing is not only spiritual in nature, it's an act of faith. So, be sure you're bringing faith into the process.

I had one soul-sensing student who got angry with me when, during a private session, I asked him some of the preceding control-issue questions. He demanded to know what they had to do with afterlife communications. I explained that they help to determine one's ability to let go and open up to the process of soul sensing. He nodded and, after several seconds, confessed that he had recently stopped playing tennis with his lifelong friends because he was not winning as often as he once had.

"Tennis is just one more thing in my life that I can't control anymore," he added.

"But it's only a game," I replied." It's not as if you're a professional tennis player and your income depends upon how well you do at it." I was silently amazed that what should have been a fun outing with old friends was such a serious matter to him. I wondered when he had lost the sense of play he had possessed as a child. I even suggested to him that perhaps this was simply a time in his life when the universe was trying to help him be happy for his friends when they had a winning day on the court. But this supposition merely caused him to look at me as though I had lost my mind.

I'll go into more detail later in this book about how and why play and creative activities enhance our mediumistic abilities; but, for now, suffice it to say that it wasn't until I finally persuaded this student to play some tennis without keeping track of his score that his soul-sensing efforts began to produce results.

Sometimes going hand-in-hand with doubt and control issues is negativity to the point of anger. Again, I'm not sure why anyone would go into a soul-sensing or medium session with a surly attitude, but some people do. That said, I have to tell you that you're not going to get far at communicating with the dead when you're in a snippy or defiant mood. Our emotions play a key role in how our subatomic matter interacts with disembodied souls. The dead seem to respond well to just about every sentiment, except anger (and a specific type of fear, which I'll describe in a minute). This is probably because these emotions can shut down our chakras, making us less able to send and receive afterlife messages. They also compress our subatomic selves, making them less airy and more closed to transmissions from others. So, before beginning an afterlife- communication session, always shut your eyes and picture your soul: that light-emitting, subatomic essence deep within you. Then concentrate on making it as open and receptive as possible.

We all have doubts and control issues. We all get angry, and we generally know when anger is what we're feeling. However, the next big soul-sensing blocker I want to discuss can be much more insidious. It's fear, specifically *fear of the dead*. This is, obviously, not the same fear that my coworker Michael felt when his plane nearly crashed on his way home from his cabin. That panicky, "help-me" kind of fear actually attracts our deceased loved ones to us. Whereas the type I'm referring to here repels them. It is ages old and so ingrained in us that we don't always realize we're experiencing it—let alone allowing it to dictate our actions.

Fear of the Dead

If you've ever worn black to a funeral, you were carrying out an act, not of respect, but of fear. Our ancestors, going back eons, wore black when burying their dead in an effort to hide from the spirit world. They believed dark clothing would protect them from possession by the newly departed soul. What we might welcome today as temporary channeling by a recently passed loved one positively terrified our predecessors. They not only dressed in black, but they also concealed their faces. This accounts for the sheer, ebony veils we sometimes see widows wear at their husbands' funerals nowadays. Even though today's face veils at burials are most likely meant to hide displays of grief in public, we're still unwittingly protecting ourselves from spirit possession every time we don Halloween masks or costumes.

The 2,500-year-old holiday we now know as All Hallow's Eve was once a deathly serious business. The ancient Celts, who populated much of Western Europe, believed that October 31st was not only the last day of summer, but it was also the time when the barrier between this world and the next was at its thinnest. This meant the souls of the dead walked amongst the living on the last day of October, and the only defense against spirit possession was to mask one's face. In fact, the Celts were so vehement about this precautionary practice, that anyone caught not wearing a mask on Halloween night was assumed to be possessed and was burnt at the stake!

The Real Barriers

Do you still think fear is not the primary emotion behind our funeral practices today? Consider this:

While the tombstones we pay so dearly for nowadays are meant to commemorate our deceased loved ones, they were originally intended to make sure the dead *stayed* in their graves. These slabs of rock were heavy enough to help keep grave robbers out, but keeping the departed in the ground was actually the more important issue to our ancestors. This is substantiated by the fact that our distant predecessors often amputated a corpse's head and feet in the hope this would prevent him or her from returning home from the grave!

It's still considered by many to be unlucky to drive or walk past a cemetery. This isn't surprising, given that ancient pallbearers chose to take a convoluted route to and from the graveyard, in the hopes that their recently dead would not be able to track their way home from the burial site.

The fact that archaeologists usually find far too many nails securing the lids of ancient coffins than were needed for the task is additional evidence that our ancestors wanted their dead to *stay* interred. Thus the phrase we still use today: "Just another nail in his coffin lid."

From Fearful to Fashionable

I should note here that these fear-based funerary practices were much more typical of the Western world than the Orient. While the Celts and others were busy protecting themselves from their dead, many Eastern cultures were finding effective ways in which to communicate with them. In fact, it was not until the mid-1800s that the French brought the practice of séances and mediumship to the West.

How did the French discover them? They did it by colonizing Indochina, where the Vietnamese shared some of their ancient soul-sensing methods with their Western occupiers. Once séances became popular in Europe, some very prominent Americans also began the practice. Suddenly, it was fashionable in the U.S. to commune with the souls of the dead. Those who did were in the very good company of such illustrious Westerners as Thomas Edison, Sir Arthur Conan Doyle, and Abraham Lincoln. At the White House, the séances attended by President Lincoln and his wife were among the first recorded in Western history that represent my particular branch of mediumship: communicating with deceased loved ones as a form of grief consolation. By the time Abraham Lincoln was elected to the presidency, he and his wife had already lost two sons to death, and Mrs. Lincoln only seemed able to assuage her deep sorrow over these devastating losses by using a medium to speak to the souls of her boys. She had learned that this was doable and she did it. So, good for her!

Eventually, however, fraudulent practitioners began staging physical medium events, such as levitating objects and blowing spirit horns. As a result, almost all mediumship fell into disrepute—until the late 20th Century. Despite our renewed acceptance of it today, our fear of the dead persists in the West. So, because one of Heaven's rules of visitation is that the deceased not intentionally scare the living, we can inadvertently prevent our passed loved ones from communicating with us.

Taken By Surprise

As a medium, I've thought long and hard about unintentional scares, and I have come to the conclusion that it's not so much our dead whom we fear, but some of the ways in which they manifest themselves to us.

A case in point is a client of mine named Martha, whose husband, Jim, died a few years ago of a stroke. Jim was a prankster and sometimes brash in his dealings with others. So, in order to

The Real Barriers

remind me to make good on my promise to do a free medium session for his impoverished wife, he activated my document shredder in the middle of the night! This is unacceptable behavior at my house, and, when I received an unexpected call from his widow the next day, I told Jim as much. Martha was, of course, phoning to request the free session I had offered her a year earlier.

Jim's method of reminding me of my promise was both annoying and scary. As a professional medium, however, I know how difficult it can be for the dead to get the attention and cooperation of the living. After all, when are we less distracted, less noisy, and more right-brained than during the day? *The middle of the night.*

Nevertheless, I don't care for having everyone in my household startled awake at 2:00 a.m. by the sound of an appliance mysteriously roaring. And, when I did a medium session for Martha a couple days later, I discovered she liked being woken by her dead husband even less than I did. Instead of targeting one of Martha's appliances, however, Jim was going directly to her bed, and Martha would be jolted out of sleep by the feeling of him stroking her hair. While this is usually intended as a show of affection, Martha found it chilling.

During our medium session, I conveyed to Jim how unnerving his nightly visits were for Martha. Then I advised her to set aside some waking time in which to commune with her deceased husband. This would allow Jim at least 30 daytime minutes with his wife that were guaranteed to be quieter and less distracting than the rest of her day-to-day life. I instructed Martha to do her best to make sure she conducted this soul-sensing half hour at roughly the same time every day, so Jim could make arrangements to visit her on the earthly plane on cue. I also told her not to let her time with Jim's soul be disrupted by phone calls or other noises or interruptions.

The last time I checked with Martha, she said she and Jim were communing regularly as scheduled. This was allowing her to sleep well at night again. She has found that using a pendulum is her best means of communicating with Jim.

I, meanwhile, have made a habit of unplugging our document shredder when we're not using it. As a professional medium, however, I still have to contend with some middle-of-the-night visitations, and I would be lying if I claimed that the things that go bump in the night don't scare me. I'm sort of a clearinghouse for afterlife messages, so I don't always know who's paying me a visit or why. I'm usually able to deduce the answers within twenty-four hours though, because these events tend to precede phone calls from my clients.

Nevertheless, most of us are products of our fear-based Western lineage. We naturally find the seemingly invisible world of the subatomic startling and spooky. But, as I tell my soul-sensing students, "Always remember that the dead are people too. They've simply been stripped down to their subatomic essences." Until we begin to be more tolerant of the disembodied, we will not close the communication gap between our deceased loved ones and ourselves.

Soul-Sensing Summary

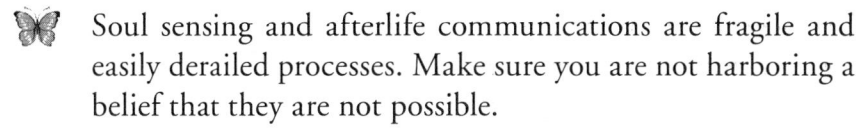

- Soul sensing and afterlife communications are fragile and easily derailed processes. Make sure you are not harboring a belief that they are not possible.

- Upon waking each morning, take a minute to ask yourself which of your soul senses you used while dreaming. Make note of what you saw, heard, felt, smelled, and tasted in your dreams. This will help get you in touch with your soul senses during your waking hours.

- Soul sensing develops slowly in some people. It takes practice and perseverance. You should try all of the communication methods provided in this book in order to find the one that works best for you.

- Our emotions and motivations play a key role in the success or failure of our afterlife communications. Anger, doubt about soul-sensing abilities, and fear of the dead are all message blockers.

- The deceased often choose to visit us in the middle of the night because that is when we are most likely to be undistracted, surrounded by quiet, and in the receptive right lobes of our brains.

- If you find nighttime visits from your dead loved ones frightening or startling, you can help redirect them by designating a quiet daytime period in which you are willing to commune with them.

- Before beginning an afterlife-communication session, always close your eyes and picture your soul: that light-emitting, subatomic essence deep within you. Then concentrate on making it as open and receptive as possible.

Chapter 5

Why & How to Protect Yourself

Lyn's Dead Friend Takes Her for a Ride

It's very unusual, thank Heavens, but sometimes I meet someone who wants protection from a deceased loved one—or, more specifically, from temporary channeling by him or her. This was the case for my dear friend, Lyn Danielson. She's been a healer and palm-reader for decades, so, perhaps she was more susceptible to temporary channeling than most people. She claimed, however, to have never even heard of it, until her longtime friend Robert died a few years ago. He was the nationally famous psychic, Robert C.H. Parker, who police employed in successfully helping to solve some of America's best-known kidnapping cases. And I can tell you firsthand that his spiritual energy was positively overwhelming when he channeled it through me, as well as Lyn, after his death.

Lyn had known Robert for many years. I, on the other hand, had only met him once, at a psychic fair. It was really a privilege for me to have made his acquaintance, because Robert rarely made public appearances. He had been badly hurt in a car accident years earlier, and this had resulted in his not being able to exercise any more. A very athletic man in his youth, the fat began to pile on after his injury, and a body weight in excess of 400 pounds, coupled with limited mobility, made it difficult for him to leave his house. His psychic abilities remained remarkably strong, however, and his name continued to be well-known due to his writings and frequent media guest spots. Naturally, whenever he did agree to offer his services at a metaphysical event, he was inundated with customers. Lyn and I were also kept busy with clients coming to us for private psychic sittings. So it was indeed a rare treat to have been able to visit with Robert when our breaks coincided one autumn afternoon at a local psychic fair.

Robert often found himself feeling nauseated after only a couple hours of doing publicly held sessions. It's not uncommon for readers at these events to report becoming headachy or just plain drained after hours of intense right-brain metaphysical communications. Some practitioners attribute this to the massive amount of psychic energy confined to one enclosed setting at such events. Ever the pragmatist, however, I tend to believe the key causes are probably stress, topped off with garden-variety dehydration. It's difficult to drink enough water when you're doing most of the talking for six hours or more. To say nothing of the wrench bathroom visits throw into the back-to-back scheduling on such occasions. Nausea, on the other hand, is not at all typical for readers under these circumstances. So, of course, I felt sorry for Robert that day, knowing he'd have to leave the gathering after just a few hours of work, because he was simply feeling too ill to continue. I felt even more sorry for all of those who wanted a one-on-one in-person session with him, but would not be able to have one.

Dead, But Not Gone

Early in January of 2008, I received an emailed newsletter from a local metaphysical community in Minneapolis. In it was an announcement that Robert C.H. Parker had died of natural causes. Lyn and I decided to attend his memorial service.

It was held on a bitterly cold day, but the setting was remarkably picturesque. Even in the dead of winter, the visitor center at our University of Minnesota's Landscape Arboretum is a breathtaking showplace. Before the service began, Lyn and I watched wild turkeys and pairs of other beautifully colored birds fluttering about the patio two stories below the panoramic windows of the room where the memorial was to be held. We were both blithely unaware of the subatomic handiwork our dead friend was about to put into play.

Although Robert had used his talents to help tens of thousands of people through the years, the gathering was rather small. Maybe thirty people had ventured out for his memorial service on that frigid day. Because he was a single man with no children and what remained of his blood family lived on the East Coast, almost all of us were either Robert's friends or his professional acquaintances. Sitting among us, however, were what appeared to be a family. It was composed of two elementary-school-aged children, a mom, and a grandmother.

I sensed Robert's loving presence all around us. I also felt unusually drawn to the family members, who were seated just a row ahead of Lyn and me. Late into the service, the man who was conducting it introduced the four of them to the rest of us. They had become Robert's surrogate family through the years. He had come to the aid of this single mother on more than one occasion, and they grew to think of him as a father figure—one who they loyally invited to their home on holidays and other special occasions.

I must admit that it was not a particularly sorrowful memorial service. The physical quality of Robert's life had declined so much over his last few years that I think most of us felt some relief in knowing he was no longer trapped inside such a disabled and ailing body. Nevertheless, both Lyn and I found ourselves oddly teary-eyed in response to his "adoptive" family. I didn't even know them, yet I felt strangely protective towards them. Once the service was over, I seized the opportunity to hand the young mother my business card and offer her a free medium session with Robert. I, meanwhile, overheard Lyn talking to the family's grandmother. Then, to my surprise, I saw Lyn give the elderly woman a long, heartfelt hug.

While Lyn is more outgoing than I am in groups of people, this action was out of character for her—given that these people were complete strangers to us. Unfortunately, Robert's little family looked rather uncomfortable with our inexplicable overtures, and none of them ever contacted us for further communication with their surrogate dad. I knew, even as we were talking to them, that Lyn and I had been unwittingly pulled into Robert's invisible influence. Seeing the surprised and slightly uneasy look on the young mother's face after I spoke to her, I headed off to talk to others in the room.

Lyn came and joined me in my socializing a couple minutes later, and she seemed to me to be herself again. I would later discover I was wrong about this, because, when she eventually headed home, it wasn't her house she drove to, but, to her amazement, *Robert's!*

She called me later and told me about her unintended trip to her dead friend's home. She sounded understandably upset by it and by her oddly demonstrative behavior towards Robert's old friend, the maternal grandmother of his surrogate family. "What the h--- happened?" she demanded to know.

"Robert was channeling through you," I replied.

"What do you mean 'channeling'?"

"You know, borrowing your body in order to say and do things he needed to."

"But what right did he have to do that?"

"None, probably. But you were available and easily accessible, because of your psychic abilities. So, he seized the opportunity to work through you. He got you to hug and console his old friend, something his sudden death didn't allow him to do himself. Then, as you drove home, his consciousness was still so embedded in you that you drove your car to his house, instead of your own. Maybe that was his way of helping you understand that *he* was the one channeling through you."

Such occurrences are par for the course for professional mediums. We understand how difficult it is for the dead to get their messages across to the living people they've left behind. So, we're more forgiving of the sometimes frightening, embarrassing, and mystifying situations into which channeling can put us. Even after I explained what had happened to Lyn, however, she was still disturbed by the invasive nature of it.

"Why didn't he ask my permission before doing those things through me?"

"*How* could he? Even if you had understood what channeling was, which you just said you didn't, how could he have communicated such a complex request to you? Let alone in time to catch his adoptive family before they left the gathering? That's just life, Lyn. Or should I say 'death.' Robert only had a brief window of opportunity to work in. He couldn't help that his surrogate family didn't realize it was *him* communicating through us and we ended up feeling embarrassed by it. We were just instruments of his love and generosity; so, no real harm done, right?"

"Right, I guess," she conceded. I could tell, though, that she was still somewhat peeved about it. A woman with great principles and admirable boundaries, Lyn clearly didn't like having been "taken for a ride"—even if it was by a disembodied friend she had known for years.

"Listen, if it happens again, just confront him about it," I advised. "Just say out loud, 'Robert, knock it off. I don't like being channeled through, so find another friend to conduct your unfinished business for you.'"

"O.K. I will," she agreed, sounding more satisfied.

Preventing Temporary Channeling

Had I suspected Robert would have had reason to channel through either Lyn or me after his memorial service, I could have taken steps to prevent it. I still feel no real harm was done by Robert's temporary possessions of us. If, however, such channeling is truly an abhorrent possibility to you, you can take measures to prevent it after the death of a loved one or acquaintance by cleaning and sealing your aura. Here's how:

1. Sit down at a desk or table and prop your elbows on it, with your forearms pointing upwards. Open your hands and position your palms so they're facing one another, about three inches apart.

2. Hold them in this position until you can feel an electrical charge building between them. This may take a minute or two, and it will make your palms feel warm and tingly. They should feel as if a subtle flow of electricity is traveling between them.

3. Once you're sure this charge is moving between your hands, stand up and run both of your palms down the length of your body—traveling over your sides and down the back and front of you, from the top of your head to the tips of your toes.

4. Take the electrical energy your palms gathered from your body in this process and throw it outdoors through an open window or door.

5. Sit down again at your desk or table and follow the directions in steps 1 and 2 above. When your palms have built up their charge, stand and follow the instructions in Step 3 above again. This time you should concentrate on shaping and seal-

ing this electrical energy into a protective, invisible bubble around your whole body, from your head to your toes.

Your aura is now cleaned and sealed, making it nearly impossible for a disembodied soul to channel through you, at least for the next 24 hours or so. This cleansing and sealing procedure should be repeated once a day for at least a week after the death of your loved one. I should point out again, however, that preventing a spirit from temporarily channeling through you closes one of the avenues to afterlife communication with that individual.

Speaking of such avenues, after counseling Lyn on Robert's channeling, I realized I had not yet requested that he stop channeling through *me*. And, to my surprise, he saw reason to continue doing so. I had made the acquaintance of a prominent literary agent through someone I met at Robert's memorial. Even though this agent, who I'll call Ted, was unable to attend Robert's service, I was told he was a close friend of Robert's. So, in the interests of preserving Ted's anonymity, I am fictionalizing some of the information about his identity here.

The day after I made Ted's acquaintance, he phoned me for a medium session with Robert's soul. Ted was clearly missing his longtime friend Robert, and, of course, I was only too happy to "audition" for such a prominent agent by giving him a free one-hour phone appointment.

This session went very well. I was able to give Ted many correct specifics about his years-long relationship with Robert. Ted was impressed with my medium abilities and said he wanted to take me on as a client. He seemed to be a pleasant enough fellow, but, during his subsequent calls, I began to feel uneasy about him. In fact, every time I spoke to him thereafter, I literally felt nauseated. This really surprised me because, as the author of fifteen novels released by New York publishers, I've met and dealt with many literary agents through the years, and I'd never had this response to any of them.

Because I so rarely experience queasiness, I gradually began to connect these episodes with Robert C.H. Parker and his stomach ailments when he was trying to do psychic sessions in public settings.

Robert's Signature

Robert was, apparently, trying to tell me something about his old friend Ted, and it obviously was not positive. Within a few weeks of Ted wooing me as a potential client, I happened upon a trade newspaper in the writing field and my eyes immediately focused upon Ted's name in an article. My mouth fell open as I read that Ted had left the U.S., purportedly fleeing with hundreds of thousands of dollars in royalties that he should have paid out to his clients!

In all of my dealings with the Other Side, I've never been made to feel physically ill by a spirit. Yet this was clearly Robert's signature with me, his way of making me know for sure who was contacting me and warning me about Ted's suddenly shady dealings. Even though Robert's method was quite unpleasant, he had clearly done me a huge favor by steering me away from Ted.

Lyn, meanwhile, began being visited by Robert in her night dreams. This was much more acceptable to her than his temporary channeling had been. She had successfully communicated to Robert's soul that she didn't mind hearing from him, but she did not want him taking possession of her body.

Robert, having been a world-class psychic in life, had proven rather heavy-handed with his communications from the Other Side. What he did with Lyn and me, while well-intended, was akin to putting a 100-watt light bulb into a 60-watt lamp. It should be noted, too, that Lyn didn't count on Robert to read her thoughts when she requested he stop channeling through her. She asked him *aloud* to stop doing it, and so should you, if a deceased relative or friend starts to make you uncomfortable with their methods of communication.

Saying "Back Off" Aloud

Lyn had already taken the most important steps. She had learned that temporary channeling by the dead is a very real phenomenon. She had also become aware of the signs of it. The most significant of these is finding yourself acting out of character. Fortunately, her behavioral changes pointed very clearly to their source: Robert C.H. Parker, so she didn't have to spend time trying to figure out who was taking temporary possession of her. Having identified the channeling soul, she called Robert out on it, loudly and clearly.

The channeling stopped immediately, and Robert found a more acceptable way to communicate with her: in her sleep. This is the usual progression of things with a friendly soul. Only when such a spirit is trying to warn you away from a certain course of action, person, or thing, will their communication be somewhat unpleasant for you. These warnings may be unnerving or uncomfortable, but they are usually brief and very specific in nature. This is why I did not scold Robert for making me feel sick to my stomach. It was not an ongoing state. It only happened when I had contact with the person Robert was trying to warn me about. And, this reminds me of another very important point: friendly spirits often get blamed for the things unfriendly spirits do.

Friend or Foe?

Although I'm not a ghost hunter, I'm often asked by my clients to help determine the cause of haunting behaviors in their homes or those of their family and friends. The first question any medium is going to ask in assessing such a situation is "Has anyone close to you died recently?" If the answer is yes, we can begin the process of determining if that passed soul is involved in the purported ghostly activities.

Once my client lists the haunting behaviors that are occurring, we assess whether any of them match the personality of the recently deceased person or pet. Often, we determine that some of them do, but others do not. A common mistake in afterlife communications is to assume that only one soul is responsible for all of the metaphysical activity in a given setting. Many times I've found that this is not true. Generally, the more negative a spirit's behavior is, the less likely it is that said soul is that of a relative or friend. Rather, it's a stranger who's haunting your dwelling, causing one of your dearly departed to intervene on your behalf. Because you can more easily identify the soul of someone you know, however, you mistakenly assign *all* of the metaphysical activities to him or her.

A good case in point came to me a couple years ago. A new client phoned me to discuss the medium abilities of her teenage daughter, Karen. Since toddlerhood, Karen had claimed to see the spirits of the dead. She had even been able to identify deceased relatives who'd passed long before she was born. She had never been afraid of these familial spirits. They seemed to her a natural part of her Native-American lineage. She was a descendant of tribal shamans, so spirit communications came naturally to her. She was quite comfortable with her mediumistic gifts. That is, until she and her family moved to another house.

Suddenly, she was on edge when she went to bed at night. She felt presences in her room, and, even though she recognized a couple of them as her passed grandparents, she felt too frightened to sleep. She would pull the bedcovers over her head and not dare to get up in the night for any reason.

It was clear to me, upon hearing her story, that Karen was no longer just being visited by spirits, she was being *haunted*. It was also apparent that the reason for this was the change of residence.

There was a history in the home that was causing some of the spirits of its passed residents to linger there and to zero in on the person in this new family whom they sensed would notice their presence. The one thing I knew we should not do was inadvertently send Karen's familial spirits away. They were there to protect her from the vexing souls, so our cleansing of her space needed to be done with discernment.

I instructed Karen to address the souls whom she recognized: that of her grandmother and great grandfather. She was to light a white candle, address them by name and tell them aloud that she knew they were there to guard her. She should also tell them they were welcome to visit her. But she was to inform them that she would be taking some metaphysical steps to rid the house of the other spirits present.

Bad Spirits Be Gone!

Once that was explained to her familial souls, Karen and her mom would begin a process that I call "the works." They were going to throw the book at those who were haunting Karen and taking advantage of her fledgling medium abilities. Because Karen and her mother were of Native American descent, most of the steps I recommended did not surprise them. Their culture had taught them to be much more aware of the workings of the spirit world than the average family in America is. Should you find that some of what I recommend sounds like bunk, please bear in mind that the subatomic world of spirits is very different from our physical plane. Subtle changes that you and I probably wouldn't even notice in our environments can be as repellant to ghosts as teargas is to the living.

The first thing I had Karen and her mother do was cleanse their new home with a sage-burning ceremony. Here are the steps I recommend for this:

1. Get a handful of loose, ceremonial (not commercial) white sage, an earthenware container with a handle, and a box of matches.
2. Shut off all noises and distractions in the space you wish to clear. Turn off communication devices, such as televisions, radios, iPods®, and cell phones, so you can concentrate fully on the ceremony.
3. Remove all clutter from a table or desktop, so you can use it to put the sage in the earthen container and light fire to it. As the sage begins to burn, take a deep breath. While you slowly release it, clear your mind of all negative thoughts and picture a positive outcome to your cleansing ceremony. If you are not conducting this ceremony alone, make sure all participants are optimistic about its outcome. No skepticism or negative remarks should be allowed. Also, this ceremony should not include babies or small children, since smoke is involved.
4. As the smoke from the sage begins to rise, pick up the earthen container by its handle and use your free hand to fan the smoke outward to all corners of each room you walk through.
5. Envision yourself and all other participants being surrounded by a protective golden light.
6. Say a prayer out loud that asks God or the Universe for purification and protection. Keep repeating this prayer in a normal speaking voice, while you move from room to room.
7. Direct the smoke towards each of the walls and around the frames of all doors and windows. Then, in each doorway, gently wave the container in a zigzag pattern, from an upward position to a downward one.

Safety precautions: Do not leave the burning sage unattended. Do not inhale the smoke directly. Ceremonial sage should not be consumed: Do not eat it or use it in food.

The next thing I asked Karen to do was begin wearing an amethyst necklace at night. This stone is generally affordable and has spiritually protective powers. I also told her to put splashes of fringe about her bedroom. Gypsies, a race famous for their clairvoyant abilities, have known for centuries that fringe and ribbon tails have clarifying abilities. This is why Gypsies are so often depicted wearing shawls and other fringe-trimmed garments and holding ribbon-adorned tambourines. Something about fringe jams communications on the subatomic level, making it too frustrating for ill-intended spirits to consistently manifest themselves in such a space.

Karen and her mom could definitely relate to this suggestion, as many of their tribal costumes were fringe-trimmed, though they had never realized that spirit-control might be one of the primary reasons for this. It's important to note, however, that fringe should always be suspended to have maximum metaphysical effect. Fringe on throw pillows, for instance, will never have the protective influence that a fringed shawl thrown over the back of a chair has.

Along with putting fringed items in her room, I suggested that Karen place a couple of vases of naturally "fringed" artificial flowers throughout it. Mimosas, Gerbera, and thin-petaled Chrysanthemums are all ideal for this purpose.

Within just a day or two of Karen taking these cleansing and spiritual steps, she told me the negative spirits had disappeared. This is the case for the vast majority of people who use these protective methods.

Michael to the Rescue

Once in a very great while, however, negative spirits continue to haunt a particular setting. When that happens, it's time to again consider the subatomic nature of disembodied souls, as I explained it in Chapter 3. Because spirits can be in two places at once, they are not bound by the same laws of time and space as the living are. Very often, a ghost who's haunting a home still thinks it's his or her property. This may also explain why ghosts are so rarely spotted in additions to homes. If they did not occupy said space when they were alive, they are not likely to spend any time there in death.

In short, based on the quantum physics I've studied, I believe we are not so much "haunted" in certain dwellings, as we are simply temporally trespassed upon. Time is not nearly as linear as the living perceive it to be. Thus the dead occasionally slip into our time and space, and we sometimes slip into theirs.

That said, if you continue to experience haunting activities in your home, even after taking the cleansing steps I gave to Karen, it's probably time for stronger measures. You should engage the services of experienced ghost hunters, who know how to make it clear to unwanted spirits that they are no longer welcome in this time and space.

In very extreme cases, Catholic priests or other ordained clergy can be called upon to cast out malevolent spirits from your space. One of the strongest of their practices is to invoke the Archangel Michael. Michael has been called upon to deal with some of the most famous haunting situations and possessions in history, and he has succeeded in setting matters right. To learn more about this Archangel and his infallible protective powers, I recommend you read these books: *The Archangel Michael: His Mission and Ours* by Rudolf Steiner and Christopher Bamford. *Spirit Guides & Angel Guardians: Contact Your Invisible Helpers* by Richard Webster.

Soul-Sensing Summary

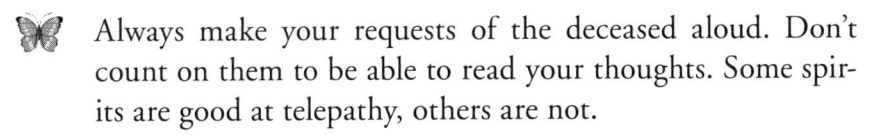

- Always make your requests of the deceased aloud. Don't count on them to be able to read your thoughts. Some spirits are good at telepathy, others are not.

- After the death of someone close to you, be aware of changes in your behavior and that of your friends and relatives. If you don't want such a disembodied soul channeling through you, clean and seal your aura on a regular basis.

- Because they come to protect you from unfriendly spirits, the souls of your deceased family and friends sometimes get blamed for haunting activities.

- Most hauntings can be ended by: conducting a sage-burning ceremony, wearing an amethyst, and putting fringe-trimmed items throughout your living space.

- Persistent hauntings sometimes require procuring the in-person help of professional ghost hunters or clergy, as well as the Archangel Michael.

"Earth hath no sorrow that Heaven cannot heal."
— Thomas Moore

Chapter 6

Getting Your Right Brain Right

How I Taught Dr. Laura Kroeten-Bue to Pierce the Veil

Peter Bue and Jack had been friends for decades. So, when Peter died of a heart attack at the age of 54, Jack took a bold step to help console Peter's widow, Laura: he hired me to do a medium session for her.

Laura Kroeten-Bue had never met a medium. She wasn't even sure what to expect from afterlife communications. Yet, if you asked her today, I'm certain she'd tell you that medium appointment from her husband's friend was one of the best gifts she's ever received. She had come to the session not to say the good-bye her husband's sudden heart attack had precluded, but "Hello, again, Peter. We're now able to be back in touch."

Peter, a very dynamic spirit, came through with incredible strength and clarity during that first appointment, and he's been communicating with Laura every month since! Unlike most of my clients, who have a session with me once or twice a year, Laura wanted appointments at least twice a month. Because I keep my fees low, she can afford them. Ordinarily, I would have warned Laura against having medium sessions so often, but she was about to receive her doctorate in psychology, so I figured she knew about the dangers of displacement (the unconscious transference of affection from one person to another). It's rare, but mediums do need to be aware that serving as the mouthpiece of a deceased individual can lead to a client coming to think of that medium as *being* that dearly departed person. That's why it's important to teach repeat clients some ways in which to do medium work on their own. I, therefore, began fairly early on to tell Laura how to develop her soul senses, so she could receive and send messages to Peter directly.

Left, Logical, Linear

The first challenge with this was that Laura, a nurse and psychologist, was predominantly left-brained. People who function almost exclusively in their left brains during their workday often have more difficulty engaging in afterlife communications than more creative, right-brained types.

None of us choose to be primarily left- or right-brained. Rather, we're born with a tendency to be stronger in one or the other of our brain's hemispheres. The findings of evolutionary science point to the likelihood that humankind was originally right-brained, and we developed left brains as the need for using tools and language arose. This change marked the shift from our Garden-of-Eden fruit-gatherer stage to sweat-of-our-brows hunting with handmade weapons, in order to scrape out steady livelihoods for ourselves. Not surprisingly, our left brains have been guiding us through our workdays ever since. The left brain enables us to engage in sequential and linear thinking, so we can follow directions and carry out tasks in the most logical, efficient manner.

Determining Your Dominance

Consider, for instance, how you give others directions to a location. If you say things like, "Drive west three miles and turn north on Maple Street," you are probably a mainly left-brained person. If, on the other hand, you phrase directions like this, "Drive that way [pointing], until you reach the intersection with the McDonald's. Then take a right and keep going till you pass the big shopping center on your left."—you're primarily a right-brained person.

The right-brained are into visual cues, such as landmarks, rather than the more mathematical process of keeping track of miles traveled on an odometer.

Here's a quiz to take to help you determine which side of your brain is dominant for you. Simply circle the answer that applies most to you after each statement.

1. I have to write appointment times and tasks down on a calendar in order to remember them.
   True   False

2. I'm almost always very aware of what time it is.
   True   False

3. Before beginning a project or assignment at work, I need to know why I'm doing it or what the ultimate goal is with it.
   True   False

4. I'm an out-of-sight-out-of-mind person, needing visual prompts or cues to remind me what needs to get done and in what order.
   True   False

5. I get bored with doing tasks in order of priority. I prefer to do what feels most interesting to me at any given time.
   True   False

6. When someone asks me to recount an occurrence, I use my hands and image-filled description, rather than just words, to do so.
   True   False

7. In school, I easily got good grades in math.
   True   False

8. I tend to be analytical in my thinking.
   True   False

9. I often override my emotions, in order to appear controlled and consistent.
   True   False

10. I'm a realist, rarely indulging in wishful thinking.
    True   False

11. I try to do everything the right way.
    True   False

12. I think it's possible to manifest a joyful life for myself.
    True   False

13. When I lose one of my belongings, I'm usually able to find it by mentally picturing where I last saw it.
    True   False

14. I read the instructions before trying to assemble an appliance or piece of equipment.
    True   False

15. I tend to run late in getting to work, appointments, or social gatherings.
    True   False

16. I'm often intuitive, knowing when something significant is about to happen.
    True   False

17. Without using any psychic abilities, I would be good at solving crimes.
    True   False

18. I am very creative. I write poetry, fiction, music, or I paint, draw, sculpt or make art objects.
    True   False
19. I usually write a list of the pluses and minuses, before making important decisions.
    True   False
20. I *know* undisclosed facts about people I've just met.
    True   False

Please check out your results on this quiz by turning to the end of this chapter. If your answers indicate that you're more left-brained than right, I highly recommend you try some of the exercises in this chapter in order to develop your soul-sensing abilities.

The lists below will help you better understand the functions of your left and right brains.

Left Brain	Right Brain
Logic	Intuition
Verbal skills	Nonverbal skills (using imagery, not just words)
Conscious processing	Subconscious processing
Literal interpretations	Symbolic interpretations
Realistic thinking	Fantasizing **(daydreaming & night dreaming)**
Control, consistency	Emotions, reactions
Mathematical, scientific tasks	**Artistic, musical, dramatic skills**
Linear, sequential thinking/tasks	Wholistic thinking (Filling gaps with intuition)
Temporal awareness	Lack of temporal awareness (Cannot sense time)
Judgment, evaluation	Nonjudgmental, uncritical thinking

As you can imagine, those in the composing arts spend many of their waking hours in their right brains. Other occupations tend to require mainly left-brain skills. You may have noticed in Chapter 1 that I mentioned I'm the author of fifteen novels issued by New York publishing houses. That might have seemed just incidental, when, in fact, it's the main reason I was able to become a medium. Had I been a full-time bookkeeper when I met Tjody Jacobsen, her mother would not have found me nearly as receptive to her soul's messages. Why? Because bookkeeping, along with most other kinds of work we do in our day-to-day lives, is a left-brain activity.

Right-brained people tend to be creative and intuitive, usually choosing to listen to gut feelings, rather than logic. When you do something creative, you switch over to your right brain and that's the lobe you need to strengthen in order to develop your soul senses.

Play At It

It surprises most people to learn that they don't really have to *work* to develop their soul senses, they have to *play* in the creative ways children do. One of my first questions to those who wish to communicate with deceased loved ones is, "What do you do that's creative?"

They usually look taken aback and answer, "Nothing." And I'll say, "Really? You don't scrapbook, sew, bead, decorate cakes, or write in a journal? Don't you have any hobbies that are creative?" Most people can say yes to this, if they really think about it. To those who cannot, though, I reply, "Well, start creating right away! Just dedicate an hour or two a week to it, if that's all the time you can spare. You'll have fun. It will help you relax. And you'll be developing your soul senses, all at the same time."

The Composing Arts

Go buy a candle-making kit and add your own original touches to your wax creations. Start finger painting. Decorate a cake or a sweatshirt. Come up with something completely new in any area of inventiveness which catches your fancy. What you create doesn't have to be perfect or even good. It's the sheer act of making it that matters most in this case.

Have fun, but be sure it's a creative endeavor, not a performing one. By that I mean you need to engage in the *composing* arts: writing music, fiction, or poetry, designing pottery, jewelry, etc. I'm not talking about the performing arts, such as singing, dancing, acting, or reciting someone else's poetry. You actually have to *create* something. For instance, come up with the steps and moves for an all-new dance routine, rather than performing one that somebody else choreographed.

Unfortunately, Peter was the only artist in the Bue marriage. Although I suggested it, Laura didn't seem interested in undertaking creative activities. When I met her, she had a doctorate thesis to write and lots of paperwork to deal with, due to her husband's sudden death. This meant I had to think of another way for her to access her right brain during her waking hours.

Journaling

Laura had started out tape-recording our medium sessions, but she gradually began recording the details of them in a handwritten journal. This gave me the opportunity to suggest that she add to this diary by writing messages to Peter in it. Amazingly, even though I didn't know what questions she was writing in her journal, we discovered that Peter's responses to them would come through me during my medium sessions with Laura. Peter was obviously receiving his wife's written communications, but the ultimate goal was to get Laura to a point where she could not only send messages to him, but receive them as well. This called for a few very specific steps:

1. Laura's journaling would have to be contained in a small, portable notebook, which she could carry in her purse or coat pocket. She would need to take it almost everywhere she went. Nine years of full-time novel writing has taught me that creativity, divine intervention, and messages from the Other Side tend to strike when we're keeping our critical left brains busy with workaday activities. So, Laura had to be prepared to write down fleeting impressions, words, and images from Peter, while she was riding the bus to her nursing job, taking a lunch or coffee break, or even buying groceries.

The spirits of our passed loved ones are attracted by the physical elements of life: water, air/wind, earth, and fire. Thus, these souls are notorious for sending messages to us while we're showering, driving a car, gardening, or sitting with family or friends near a glowing hearth. In short, their messages often come when we're least able to write them down. So, keeping your portable journal close at hand is the only way to assure you won't forget something important.

2. Laura would have to begin to determine which words and images were actually from Peter and which were simply the products of her own memories, daydreaming, or imagination. While it is very common for a dead loved one to reminisce with the living about happy times they shared with us on Earth, bona fide messages from the Other Side tend to have an out-of-the-blue quality that will indicate they came from a source outside of your own mind. It's not unusual, for instance, to have a memory of a fun family outing flood your brain when you're looking at a photo album of that time in your life. However, when such a memory flashes into your head while you're doing something entirely unrelated, it's the

mark of spirit communication. If you find yourself saying, "Wow! I haven't thought about that in years," and there's no external reason why you would now, someone is definitely popping in on you from the Other Side.

Afterlife messages also tend to be recurrent. Just as we, the living, will repeat something we've uttered, if we believe the person we said it to did not hear or comprehend it, so the deceased often repeat a word or image, if it's important to get it across to a living loved one.

3. Laura would have to realize that even fleeting images can form into messages. So, she would have to put pen to paper, even if it was only a single word, a doodle, or a seemingly senseless phrase that popped into her head. Given some time to reflect upon it, even a fragment of a message might come to make sense to her.

Personal Meanings

A great example of this occurred many years ago, when I was first testing my medium abilities on family and friends. My longtime confidante, Carole Nelson Douglas, a well-known mystery novelist, agreed to let me try my hand at doing an afterlife-communication session between her and a recently deceased associate of hers. This was a woman I had never met and about whom I knew nothing.

As I began the reading, I saw an image of a purple gown. I told Carole this, but it just didn't ring a bell for her. As far as Carole could recall, neither she nor her dead friend had ever owned a purple gown or even worn one. Nevertheless, this image remained in my mind the whole time I was bringing through verifiable information to Carole from her friend. Finally, a voice inside me said, "Try harder, Janice. What does a purple gown mean to you personally?"

I searched my mind for an answer. Purple symbolized royalty to me. A gown is, of course, more formal than a dress and usually floor-length. So, who wore a purple gown? My thoughts raced back to my first memories of such a garment. When I was about four years old, my adoptive mother had shown me a magazine photo of Queen Elizabeth II's coronation attire. While her gown was white, the royal robe she donned just after the ceremony was made of rich purple velvet. Then, thank Heavens, my right brain finally made the symbolic leap for me.

"Was your deceased friend named *Elizabeth*?" I asked Carole.

"Yes," she exclaimed. "Never Liz or Beth or any shortening of that name. Always 'Elizabeth.' She was a formal person and very particular about what others called her."

I can sometimes have trouble bringing through names from the Other Side. I usually get the first initial of a name right, but Carole's friend Elizabeth was obviously determined to have me bring through her name intact. All of this to say that every piece of information you receive may be significant, no matter how vague or irrelevant it may seem at first.

Getting back to Laura Bue, however: she was on board with the three specifics of journaling. She kept her notebook with her as much as possible. She was demonstrating a good sense of what were legitimate messages from Peter versus her own thoughts and reflections. She also worked regularly with me to sort out the images which both she and I received when communicating with him. Nevertheless, she was still too tentative and nonspecific in gathering and interpreting soul-sensing information. She would, for example, mention receiving a vision of a particular color from Peter, but then she couldn't bring through anything more to help fit it into some kind of context. She would talk about experiencing a certain sensation from him, such as shortness of breath—but she was unable to tell me if this should be attributed to a past event, like Peter's heart attack, or some future happening he was trying to foretell. She didn't seem able to fill in the gaps in the information Peter was giving her with either her intuition or with left-brained logic. In short, she still was not spending enough of her waking hours in her right brain.

A Different Kind of Meditation

I suggested she start meditating on a regular basis. Because this would only require a few minutes per day, she agreed to try it. Be advised, however, that the meditation I recommend for promoting medium communications is different from the garden-variety type most people do for the purposes of relaxation.

Any kind of meditation can be difficult, at first, because it involves stilling your body and quieting your mind. Sounds a little like being asleep, right? You have to do it while you're awake, however, and that's what makes it tricky.

All types of meditation start with these three steps:

1. Getting quiet
2. Getting comfortable
3. Getting focused

Getting quiet means not only quieting your mind, but shutting down the noise around you. Turn off your TV, radio, and any other sounds in your environment. Obviously, it's best to meditate when you're alone or can, at least, be left alone. If you've got noisy family members or neighbors, try using headphones or ear-buds when meditating. You might choose a white-noise tape to listen to in order to block out the sounds around you. Listening to recordings of drumming or repetitive, percussive music is an even better choice for medium meditation. In this way, you give a heartbeat back to your deceased loved one. This sort of rhythm can summon the passed party you seek in much the same way that fire, wind, water, and soil do.

Do not choose music with lyrics, however. Deciphering words is a left-brain skill, and the goal of medium meditation is to get into your right brain and stay there for several minutes.

A Vacation for Your Mind

Unless we stop them, our brains automatically race to all of the left-brain things we have to do in the upcoming day: our 9-to-5 jobs, errands, cooking, cleaning, child care, pet care—you know the list. In fact, most of us wake up with it marching through our heads every morning. That's why meditation is so important. It allows us to steal a few minutes away from all of our day-to-day demands. It's a vacation for the mind, and I hope you'll come to view it not as just another must-do, but as something you enjoy—your own private trip to the peace and wisdom of the Other Side.

It's crucial to be physically comfortable while you're meditating. Choose a cushy piece of furniture to sit on; but don't meditate lying down. A reclining position can too easily lead to falling asleep, which may cause you to be late for all of your daily obligations. For this reason, I also recommend setting a timer to let you know when your designated meditation time has ended.

As for getting focused, begin by paying attention to your breathing. Breathe in slowly to the count of four. Then exhale gradually to the count of four. After doing this a couple times, press a finger to the outer side of your left nostril to close it. Then inhale and exhale through your right nostril only. This will help stimulate your right brain.

I Scry

Your next object of focus will be a scrying bowl. This is a clean earthenware or baked-clay bowl filled halfway to the rim with fresh water. Set it on a table in front of you. Or, if you prefer, sit on the floor and place the bowl between your legs, so you can comfortably stare down into it.

This type of meditation is meant to cultivate your clairvoyant abilities. It helps you gather images from the Other Side which you can then piece into messages. This method has been used by mediums since ancient times, with its origins in Greece. The use of the life-giving elements of water and earth (in the form of your earthen bowl) help amplify your deceased loved one's ability to send you images. Make a mental note of anything that appears to you in the bowl. Then jot it down when your session is over. It's best not to interrupt your meditative state in order to write about any images you see, because the physical act of writing is a left-brain skill. For this reason, you may want to describe any images you see into a tape recorder.

A similar medium method is the psychomanteum or "mirror gazing." Also known as an apparition booth, this is done in a small darkened room or closet. Letting little or no light into the room, sit in a comfortable chair before a large, free-standing or wall mirror and gaze into it for several minutes. In most cases, the gazer begins to see an image or images in the mirror.

Admittedly, this method is too spooky for me. I don't like staring at anything in the dark, unless I'm stargazing or visiting a planetarium. Nevertheless, Dr. Raymond Moody, author of *Life After Life,* used the psychomanteum in his research following hundreds of subjects seeking reunions with deceased loved ones, and he concluded that it was useful in healing grief. Part of the success of the psychomanteum method is, undoubtedly, the sensory deprivation it imposes. If total darkness would unnerve you in such an endeavor, however, you might want to try adding the flickering light of a single candle to it. Archaeologists have concluded that, when the ancient Greeks used this method, it was done in a cave or darkened maze wherein there were probably lit torches or oil lamps, so firelight should not compromise its effectiveness.

Automatic Writing

Once Laura was meditating on a regular basis, she could expand her journal entries about Peter to include some automatic writing. This is a technique in which you meditate for a few minutes, then you write down anything that pops into your mind. Don't worry about forming whole sentences or whether what you're writing makes sense. The right brain is a nonjudgmental lobe, so don't criticize what you write. Don't pay any attention to the part of your left brain that says things like "That's the wrong word" or "That's not how that's spelled." This is not the time to edit, but just to write.

To help assure you're not being critical of your automatic writing, try doing it with your eyes shut. The more you do this, the more you'll begin to sense that the deceased loved one you seek is channeling through you and making your hand write the words and messages he or she wishes to convey.

Automatic Drawing

When I bring through messages from Peter to Laura, he often prefers to converse with me via automatic *drawing*. What more perfect means of communicating for a professional artist and painter like Peter? The only problem with it is that I can't draw my way out of a paper bag! And Laura says she doesn't draw well enough to even attempt it. Then again, she has so many of Peter's masterful paintings around her that it's probably impossible for her to feel equal to the task of drawing *anything*. Nevertheless, to the extent to which my pathetic doodling captures what Peter means to draw, it has proven to be a viable means of mediumship for me.

I have facilitated afterlife communications for thousands of spirits and their living loved ones through the years, so it's interesting to me that Peter is the only soul who has moved me to do automatic drawing. Of course, being primarily clairaudient, I gather most of his messages with my inner ear. Yet he still manages to convey a lot of information by compelling me to draw. When Laura and I do our sessions, my note pad becomes splashed with childlike depictions of flowers, people, animals, household objects, and just about anything else Peter wishes to discuss with his widow. However simplistic, my automatic drawings are good enough for me to describe them to Laura during our phone sessions and for her, in turn, to deduce what Peter means by them. They are usually references to what has most recently happened in Laura's life or those of their two grown daughters.

Peter will have me draw a certain kind of food, for instance, and then I'll discover from Laura that she has eaten it within the past day or so. He may move me to sketch a garment or accessory, whereupon Laura will confirm that she has recently purchased or worn something matching my picture. These are the ways in which Peter assures his wife and daughters that he is still a part of their day-to-day lives and that he continues to share in their earthly experiences.

What You See Is What They Mean

Most mediums would agree that you should start by taking any image you receive literally. That is to say that, if Peter has me draw a couple of peaches, he probably means actual pieces of the fruit we all know as peaches. Nevertheless, this is where you, the client, have the absolute advantage over a medium who is trying to help you with afterlife communications. When I told Laura that I had received such an image during one of our sessions, she corrected me and said, "No. Peter doesn't mean real peaches. He means our daughters' childhood friend 'Peaches,' who just got back into town the other day and came to visit us. His real name isn't 'Peaches,' of course. That's just a nickname the girls gave him. His name is actually James."

It's just this sort of double or hidden meaning that makes it necessary for professional mediums to remember to convey precisely the images they are shown by the deceased and not indulge the urge to add too much self-interpretation to them. Had I, instead, said to Laura, "You've been eating peaches lately," rather than "Peter's showing me peaches. What does that mean?"—she might not have picked up on Peter's reference to his having witnessed his daughters' reunion with their longtime friend.

Two other stunning examples of this have occurred recently during my afterlife-communication sessions with Laura and Peter. The first was that Peter had me draw the kind of pronged-branches one might see serving as "arms" on a snowman. I told Laura about this image, content to think it referred to her recently having seen a snowman. She informed me, however, that Peter was, in fact, acknowledging his youngest daughter's nickname for him: "Skeletor hands."

Then, just a moment later, Peter showed me normal human hands squeezing a tomato until it burst into a runny red mess. According to Laura, this had nothing to do with someone actually squishing a tomato. Rather, it was Peter's follow up to the last image he'd brought through. Laura instantly knew what this description meant: Peter's nickname for his youngest daughter, in turn, was "Catsup Girl," because of her tendency to put catsup on almost everything she eats.

Past Or Present?

In addition to all Peter says about Laura's present life, he often talks about their experiences together when he was still physically alive. Like all of us, he refers to current and past events when he speaks. Unfortunately, time telling is the hardest part of mediumship. The right brain doesn't gauge time well. So, again, a client like Laura has the decided advantage over her professional medium. A great example of this occurred just a few months ago, when I was doing a session with Laura. "Peter is showing me a picture of your oldest daughter on a TV Guide. What does this mean? Did she make it onto a reality show or something?"

Laura laughed. "No. Years ago, when she was nine or ten, Peter painted a mockup of a TV Guide cover. Then he added her face to it. You know. To give her a thrill, like 'you're the star of the week, sweetheart.'"

Once Laura explained this to me, it made total sense. Peter's paintings often captured this type of pop culture. Creating incredibly precise paintings of modern celebrities was his specialty. Without Laura's participation in this afterlife communication, however, I would not have realized he was referring to an event which happened over a decade earlier.

Image Downloads

In addition to his commentary on his family's past and present, Peter also indicates that he can tune into his wife's thoughts. I'll often tell Laura about an image I'm receiving from Peter only to hear her say, "I was just thinking about that today!" It's not typical for spirits to be able to read the thoughts of the living, but Peter and Laura were married for over two decades and they are still soul mates. All this to say that, once you begin receiving telepathic messages from your deceased loved one, it becomes possible for you to graduate beyond the medium's language of images and symbols to having dialogs with him or her in your head.

This happened to me recently, when I received word of the death of an old family friend. Suddenly, my mind was filled with an amazingly vivid stream of all of the unique features of her house on Lake Minnetonka. I even saw her two long-dead German

Shepherds, whom she assures me have been reunited with her in Heaven. These forty-year-old images zipped through my mind in such an exhilarating rush that I found myself awestruck. I thought I had forgotten about them, but our old friend Barbara brought them back to the fore of my brain as if I were just seeing them for the first time. I whispered my profound thanks that Heaven had brought such a joyful, indomitable role model into my life when I was a young girl.

Barbara, like Peter, was a person who lived life to the fullest until the day she died and who always overcame boredom and drudgery with creativity and resolution. Both Barbara and Peter seem determined to make certain that we, the living, can one day make the transition to Heaven with a sense of anticipation rather than fear—knowing that death is only another step in the evolution of our souls. So, it's with their kind assurances that I promise you, if you practice the form of meditation I've described in this chapter, you, too, will eventually experience this wonderful type of afterlife telepathic communication with a loved one.

Peter's Predictions

Because the dead are not functioning in the realm of time, they can also give us messages about the future. While most medium sessions with the deceased are not intended to generate prophetic information, Laura and I started to notice that Peter would sometimes send images during a session that did not pertain to the present or the past. Laura would then check with her daughters to determine whether the information related to either of them. When both claimed it did not, Laura and I would have to write it off as what we mediums call a "miss." This is an incorrect or irrelevant message that may have been caused by a variety of problems on the receiving end. Misses are most often the result of a medium misinterpreting or over interpreting a message or image. They can also be caused by what I refer to as "channel drift," as with radio transmissions. If two or more spirits are speaking at once or, if the spirit "frequency" you're on drifts into another afterlife-communication channel, messages naturally become confused or garbled. Because this didn't happen very often with Peter and me, Laura seemed content to ignore it. That is *until* such seemingly impertinent messages turned out to be predictions of future events!

In one instance, Peter told me that one of Laura's close relatives was about to marry. However, both Laura and her daughters claimed to know nothing of any wedding plans in the pipe. Then, weeks later, Laura informed me that one of her family members had indeed eloped and kept it a secret from her immediate family for months.

Once Laura and I realized Peter was able and willing to impart some future events to us, we noticed that he became more exact about them. "When you go to Europe, you will meet someone famous," he had me tell Laura, before she went on vacation abroad.

Peter was a painter of some note. His art is part of the Minnesota Historical Society's collection and his work has recently won the interest of the Weisman Museum. So, I thought it likely that Peter had some well-known contacts in the art world. Just for clarification, therefore, I asked Laura if she or her daughters knew of any such contacts in Europe. Laura assured me they did not. Yet, when she returned from their trip to France and Italy a few weeks later, she phoned me and excitedly announced that, through a series of unexpected events, she and her daughters had been allowed to meet Pope Benedict XVI!

This serendipitous encounter had come about due to a casual conversation Laura had with a British acquaintance, named *Peter*, just outside the Coliseum. He happened to have passes to a prayer service at the Vatican. He offered them to Laura, and, being a devout Catholic, she gladly accepted them. This resulted in Laura and her daughters coming within just a few feet of the Pope and being personally blessed by him during the service.

This future-events messaging continued with Peter and eventually led to him foretelling world happenings. That, however, is a subject that has proven so momentous that it really deserves a book all its own. Suffice it to say that, as of this writing, Peter has made 33 correct predictions of world events. You can view some of these on my website: www.JaniceCarlson.com.

In any case, I'm very happy to report that Laura has progressed in her afterlife communications with Peter to a point where he not only witnesses her earthly life, but sometimes temporarily transports her spirit to his current plane of existence in Heaven. This has been the result of Laura's persistence in developing her two strongest soul senses: clairvoyance and clairsentience. Monitoring her meditation sessions and her night dreams has proven key for her in all of this.

As with most endeavors, you'll find that fine-tuning the afterlife-communication process requires experimentation and practice. In time, you, too, will discover the soul-sensing methods that work best for you.

Results of Left-brain, Right-brain Quiz: If you answered "True" to questions 1, 3, 4, 5, 6, 12, 13, 15, 16, 18, 20, your right brain is dominant. If you answered "True" to questions 2, 7, 8, 9, 10, 11, 14, 17, 19, you are more left-brained.

Soul-Sensing Summary

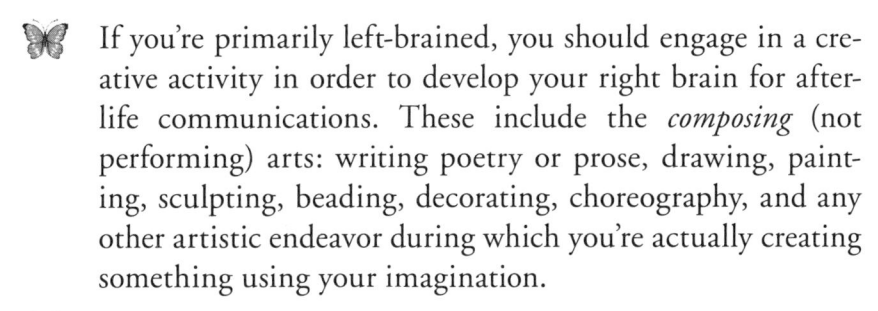

- If you're primarily left-brained, you should engage in a creative activity in order to develop your right brain for afterlife communications. These include the *composing* (not performing) arts: writing poetry or prose, drawing, painting, sculpting, beading, decorating, choreography, and any other artistic endeavor during which you're actually creating something using your imagination.

- Another way to improve your soul-sensing abilities is to meditate. Medium meditation includes focusing upon a scrying bowl or mirror or using an "apparition booth."

- After meditating, make note of any images you received during it. These images can often be pieced together to form messages.

- Bona fide messages from the Other Side tend to have an out-of-the-blue quality that will indicate they came from a source outside your own mind.

- Afterlife messages, especially if initially ignored, tend to be recurrent. Your dearly departed will often repeat them until you acknowledge them.

- Although there are general meanings that mediums associate with certain images, *you* will always be the most effective interpreter of the images your loved one sends you.

- Your deceased loved ones are capable of conveying messages about current events in your life, reminiscing about past times they've spent with you and even predicting future happenings.

Chapter 7

Soul Sensing With Your Chakras

Just as our deceased loved ones are composed of an energy that most closely resembles light, we, the living, have light within our bodies. An entire spectrum of it, in fact. We are walking, talking rainbows, from the deep red of our root chakras, at the base of our spines, to the violet of the chakras at the crowns of our heads. Founded in the ancient Hindu faith, the existence of the seven major human chakras has been confirmed by present-day science's discovery that these energy points function at a higher electromagnetic-gauge-symmetry level than the rest of our bodies.

The truth, however, is that most Westerners pay no attention to their chakras. In fact, nine-tenths of my clients have admitted to me that they didn't even know what chakras were, until I described them and how they can be used for soul sensing. What my customers do know, though, is that they often *feel* it when a deceased loved one is visiting them. They experience tingles around the back of their necks and shoulders. Or they feel an inexplicable warmth in their midsections when they remember a cherished childhood pet. Fortunately, these seemingly ineffable sensations can be explained, monitored, and even fostered. Indeed, they are at the very crux of clairsentinence: "clear feeling." It's important to learn about your chakras because they will help you pinpoint what you're feeling and which spirit is making you feel it.

Getting to Know Your Chakras

I'll start with the most basic of basics here. The human body appears to be solid, but it's composed of atoms, which are nothing more than fast-moving energy and space. What's more, this energy is measurably higher in certain parts of your anatomy than in others.

These high-energy points include:

- The top of your head (the "Crown" chakra)
- The area between your eyebrows (the "Brow" chakra)
- Your throat, neck, jaw, mouth, and teeth (the "Throat" chakra)
- Your heart and chest (the "Heart" chakra)
- The area above your stomach and just below your diaphragm (the "Solar Plexus" chakra)
- Your pelvis (the "Sacral" chakra)
- The base of your spine (the "Root" chakra)

Our chakras serve many purposes, but the most important of these, in terms of soul sensing, is their ability to conduct, filter, and combine energies from both Heaven and disembodied spirits. The top three chakras (the crown, brow, and throat) are responsible for gathering clear-seeing, clear-hearing, clear-smelling, clear-tasting, and clear-feeling information. The middle chakras (the sacral and solar plexus) most often control our clear-watching and clear-knowing abilities. For example, one of the ways you can determine which of your deceased loved ones is visiting you is if they give you a mild indication of their cause of death. Heart-attack or lung-cancer victims may make your heart chakra feel heavy or tight. Those who died of stomach-related illnesses may make your solar-plexus area feel uncomfortable. I must stress here, though, that such sensations are usually instantaneous and they are meant only as spirit-identification signatures. They are not intended to cause you suffering or alarm.

Taking the Energy Elevator

The first step I recommend to my clients, when they begin a chakra meditation, is that they choose a quiet place where they can sit on a cushion or mat. Then they should close their eyes and begin to get better acquainted with each of their chakras. It's important to sit on the floor and not on a chair or sofa, because chakra awareness has to do, in part, with the earth's energy. So, you'll want to let it travel up through the floorboards of your home and channel into your root chakra, at the base of your spine.

If you have a physical disability that prevents you from sitting on the floor or you live in a high-rise apartment, far from the earth's grounding energy, you might want to fill a plastic bag with soil or sand and sit on it in order to amplify the energy of the earth.

As you do this exercise, you will not only become aware of each of your body's energy centers, but you will also balance them and bring them into alignment. This will not just improve your mediumistic ability, it will also contribute to your wellbeing, emotional stability, and mental clarity.

So, start by concentrating on the base of your spine, feeling a small amount of the earth's gravity and warmth travel up your back. Imagine that your spine is an elevator for this unseen surge. The second stop for this energy is right next door to your root chakra: your pelvis. Again, experience the earth's energy in this, your "sacral" chakra, which can be either a center of pleasure and productivity or closed down and afraid of advances from others.

Next, imagine this line of energy traveling up to your solar plexus. This is a chakra that you can and should monitor whenever you need what is most commonly known as a "gut check." It can either be filled with fear and indecision or bolstered with confidence in your choices and actions.

The next stop is your heart and chest. The heart chakra may feel limited and closed, or it can seem open and brimming with good will and generosity. Be sure to check your back at this level of your chest, as well. Often, when a deceased spirit wants to encourage one of your actions or thoughts, he or she will send affirmative tingles to the area around your shoulder blades.

Now, move upward to your neck and throat. Although the throat chakra does not customarily include your shoulders, most mediums will confirm that sensations there are very common when you're communicating with Heaven. Proverbial "pats on the back," as well as hugs from those on the Other Side are often felt at the shoulder level.

The next stop on your energy elevator is at the point between your eyebrows. This brow chakra is responsible for clairvoyance (clear seeing), so this is where you'll want to focus your energy when attempting to receive images from a deceased loved one.

The last stop is the top of your head or your crown chakra. In my many years of doing medium work, I've heard my clients speak of three very specific sensations of spirit visitation on this level. The first is the feeling of an unseen hand stroking their hair in a loving manner. The second is a distinct tapping sensation, as if someone is rapping on the crown of the head with a single fingertip. The third is the whisper-light feeling of static electricity drawing the hairs at the top of the head upward. This sensation can be replicated by lightly rubbing an inflated party balloon against a smooth garment you're wearing. Then hold the statically charged balloon just a quarter of an inch above the crown of your head and notice how unusual it feels to have your hair suddenly stand up on end. This is a very illuminating exercise because the subatomic form of the dead can cause them to have a touch so light it can be imperceptible to the living, unless we train ourselves to recognize the feel of it.

Now, let's take a more detailed look at each of the chakras. I'll discuss ways to make them more receptive, as well as what sorts of spirit messages you can expect to receive via each of them. Because the top three chakras are the most important to afterlife communications, we'll start with the crown chakra and move downward.

Meditating on Your Crown Chakra

Known to the Hindus as the "spiritual portal" of the body, the crown chakra is in its prime in those who are 42 years of age or older. This observation correlates with my earlier conclusion that our ties to the afterlife increase as our reproductive abilities decrease. Nevertheless, there are several ways for people of all ages to activate this very significant energy center. I recommend methods that dovetail with the crown chakra's hue, such as lighting a violet-colored candle and surrounding yourself with fragrances derived from lilacs or hyacinths. Traditional practices for energizing the crown include wearing a skullcap during meditation, listening to Indian ragas, holding an amethyst or alexandrite, and putting a drop of one of these essential oils on the scalp at the crown of your head: violet, lavender, or lotus.

Your crown chakra is the most spiritually pure of your energy points, so it is most likely to attract truly angelic energy, as well as highly evolved spirits and deceased loved ones whom you knew to be learned, disciplined, and wise. If you're in doubt about which of your passed family members or friends might be communicating with you at this chakra level, let the above description be your guide. One of them may be sagacious enough to be trying to give you suitable counsel or guidance. He or she could be attempting to protect you from ill-considered decisions on your part by literally giving you a little thump on the head. This spirit may also be endeavoring to inject Heavenly foresight into your spiritual door by offering you images of future events. If you don't recognize the visions a spirit gives you as being a reference to a current or past occurrence, it could well be a glimpse of your future.

Many of my clients, who have recently lost a parent, will tell me they have experienced strange sensations at the crowns of their heads. This is because a mother or father is likely to feel protective of their children, even when they are grown. The living may literally feel that the deceased parent is tucking them into bed at night and patting their heads, as if to say "sleep well."

Along that vein, many of my widowed clients tell me they get that same sensation of caretaking from the soul of a dead spouse. (This is not to be confused with romantic energy, however. That's an entirely different sensation in a much lower chakra.) Often experienced while in bed or when lying down, such crown chakra visits are usually meant to say simply, "I guard you when you sleep."

I recommend beginning a crown-chakra session by reclining on a bed or couch with your head hanging off the edge of it—*for several seconds only*. This will allow extra blood flow to your brain. (If you have neck problems, you may achieve the same result by lying on the floor and propping your legs up on an adjacent wall. Again, do this for several seconds only.)

Next, sit on the floor and close your eyes, as you begin to mediate on this spiritual portal. Shutting your eyes assures that all of the images that come to your mind during this session are from an inner source, so they're not simply products of physical vision. It's best to describe the images and sensations you receive into a tape recorder for later reference. That way, your meditation on your chakras is not interrupted by your having to write down the information you gather.

Blockages in the crown chakra are most often caused by dedicating too much thought to earthly concerns. So, when mediating on this energy level, clear your mind of all daily cares and pretend you are in Heaven.

Meditating on Your Brow Chakra

The brow chakra governs intuition and clear-seeing. When meditating on the brow, always begin by closing your eyes and visualizing an indigo five-pointed star. As you picture this star, let your mind's eye travel slowly to each of its points, moving clockwise. The points represent, respectively, the gifts of wisdom, discernment, imagination, intuition, and knowledge. This exercise will help to clear your inner vision, so you can better receive images and messages from your deceased loved ones.

The second step I recommend, when you're starting a brow-chakra meditation, is to lie down and place a smooth stone between your eyebrows. Because this chakra is represented by the color blue, sapphires, lapis lazuli, and tanzanite are ideal choices for this exercise. Should you not have any of these stones to place between your eyebrows, use a silver coin, because silver is the metal the ancients associated with this energy point. You may also try using a dab of Vicks® Vapor Rub or other over-the-counter substances containing camphor. The essential oils associated with this chakra are camphor, heliotrope, and sweet pea.

While some chakra guides recommend playing classical music during a brow-chakra meditation, I've found the music of Claude Debussy most stimulating, especially his famous "Clair de Lune" (Moonlight) and "Rêverie" (Daydreaming). Intended to take the listener on a wordless visual tour of a moonlit sky and landscape or to the out-of-body world of dream images, respectively, these beautiful and ingenious tunes will help enable you to see into a heavenly world far beyond our own.

Be sure to ask your deceased relative or friend to send you pertinent visuals that you may be able to piece into whole messages later. Then describe the images you see with your mind's eye into a tape recorder. Always remember that you are no novice at gathering images with your brow chakra, because you do it every night when you dream in your sleep.

In addition, try to be kind to your brow chakra during your workday, by having regular eye exams with an optometrist. Make sure your eyeglass or contact prescription is up-to-date and that you wear sunglasses as needed. Eyestrain is one of the key causes of blockages in the brow chakra.

As you begin to receive images through this energy point, do not be critical of anything your inner eye captures. Stay in the nonjudgmental right lobe of your brain, simply letting the images flow through your head, and wait to make sense of them after your meditation.

As you do this brow meditation more often, you may also begin to catch a glimpse of a deceased loved one or pet when your eyes are open. Our peripheral vision is usually the first to receive visual evidence of spirit visitation. Later, you might progress to seeing a full-on image of your deceased loved one smiling at you from across a room or standing guard in your bedroom doorway. These two are the most-often-reported spirit sightings I hear about from my clients.

Don't be discouraged if all you can physically see of your passed loved one is his or her face or just a subtle outline of a physical form. Seeing full-body images of the deceased is a very atypical experience, usually borne of a rare ability, and those who possess it often report being unable to achieve clairaudience and several of the other soul senses. I have found that experiencing smaller amounts of many soul senses is actually a more effective and informative gift, than being solely clairvoyant.

Meditating on Your Throat Chakra

The throat chakra presents an interesting dichotomy: it governs both speaking and hearing. So, if you talk too much, odds are pretty good you don't listen enough—which is a sound admonition for us all. In any case, what you do with your throat chakra will very much affect your clairaudient ability. This means, if you want to hear from your deceased loved ones via your mind's ear, you must get quiet enough, often enough to *listen* to them.

In addition, be careful about what comes out of your mouth. Lying, gossiping, and making negative comments about others are some of the key blockers of this crucial energy center. It took me decades to learn this important truth, having come from an adoptive family of criticizers. Once I finally grasped this lesson, however, I noticed that my clairaudience improved as a result. So will yours, if you make a point of diplomatically sharing your concerns with family, coworkers, and associates, rather than talking about them behind their backs. Whenever we either suppress our personal truths or fail to share them with those to whom they are pertinent, we clog this chakra. By the same token, everything we send into our throats, such as food, drink, and cigarette smoke can either aid this chakra or damage it. It follows then that overeating, poor diet, too much alcohol and, of course, smoking will all inhibit you from hearing from deceased loved ones, as well as channeling their messages and voices.

When you start a throat-chakra meditation, put on a turquoise, blue agate, or aquamarine necklace, because turquoise is the color of this energy center. The music for this chakra is opera, but, for the purposes of receiving afterlife communications, I recommend you meditate on this energy point in total silence. The messages we receive with our inner ears are often faint and it's best not to risk drowning them out with surrounding music or noise.

Then, get comfortable, relax, and shut your eyes. Picture an upside-down pyramid, which is pointing towards your heart. Once you feel centered and focused on your throat chakra, silently ask it what messages your loved ones wish to share from Heaven. Speaking these into a tape recorder for later review is ideal.

You may not think you're capable of clairaudience, but, if you've ever had a tune or a jingle playing in your mind, you're clearly able to hear what your mind's ear has to play or say. We all possess an inner voice that can either program us with positive or negative feedback. During this meditation, the messages you should pay the most attention to are those which seem to come from *outside* your stream of consciousness.

The throat chakra also governs clear-tasting and clear-smelling. So, if you've ever had the experience of smelling a deceased loved one's cologne or cigarette smoke or of inexplicably tasting a food that loved one prepared for you in the past, the throat chakra is probably your strongest energy center. It, therefore, deserves your focus. In fact, one of my clients named Joan once told me that, when meditating on this chakra, she received a visit from her maternal grandmother, who had died three decades earlier. Joan hadn't even thought about this grandma in years, so she was not seeking a message from her. Yet, as she sat, peacefully meditating on her throat chakra, her tongue perceived a flavor it had not experienced in what seemed like ages. It was the sweet, buttery taste of the cardamom bread that had been a secret recipe of that grandmother's.

Lastly, be kind to your throat chakra by avoiding long periods of talking on the phone, lengthy public speaking, or the like. Also remember to drink plenty of water during the day. Avoid excessive coughing and seek medical treatment for allergies and postnasal drip. Even the most accomplished mediums can do poorly at afterlife communications when they are physically ill with viruses, colds, or sore throats. I, for one, almost always reschedule my medium sessions if I come down with a sudden illness.

Because the throat chakra also governs the teeth and jaw, toothaches and dental problems may interfere with its receptivity. Sinus infections and earaches can also diminish your abilities with it. Of all of your chakras, the throat is the most susceptible to invasion by bacteria and viruses. Thus it's the energy center that especially requires your protection and tender, loving care.

Meditating on Your Heart Chakra

When you think of your heart chakra, picture a pink rose on a leafy stem, since both pink and green are the colors associated with it. The essential oils of this energy center are rose, carnation, and lily of the valley, so be sure to breathe in some whiffs of these lovely, sweet fragrances as you meditate on the heart chakra. You may also want to wear a copper or gold necklace with a rose-quartz or peridot pendant on it.

While breathing in to the count of four and exhaling to the count of four is helpful with all meditation, it's particularly important with this chakra, because it also governs the lungs. The ancient Hindus associated a crescent moon shape with the heart chakra, but Westerners may find it easier and more reflexive to picture a pink valentine or the aforementioned pink rose on a stem. I like to visualize this rose as just a bud at the start of this meditation. Then I envision it gradually opening to full bloom. If you do this, you will open your heart to messages and love-based miracles from Heaven. This is the chakra that governs our healing abilities and compassion for others. This stands to reason, because, until we regularly have empathy for the plights of other people, it's difficult to be in touch with our own true feelings and emotions.

This concern for the good of the masses, rather than just the few, is also apparent in the fact that the music of this energy center is choral. Imagine a choir of angels singing joyously, as this, too, is a heart-expanding experience.

When meditating on this chakra, briefly place one of your hands over your heart. As you do this, imagine your heart being one with the divine heartbeat of all creatures and people in Heaven. This will serve as a reminder that we are all connected, whether in the afterlife or here on Earth. It helps dissolve the illusion of your separateness from others, as well as the mistaken belief that physical death permanently removes our loved ones' souls from ours.

The heart chakra is notorious for contracting and even shutting down when we experience trauma and grief. So, your regular efforts to open yours will greatly aid you in receiving messages from those who have passed. When we consider the ancient heart-chakra advice to choose friends who warm our hearts, we are also reminded to pay attention not only to our deceased friends and relatives, but to those who are still physically alive.

After sufficient time has passed since the death of a spouse or significant other, I may, in some cases, recommend that my client's heart-chakra meditations include a visualization of opening the heart to the possibility of finding another suitable spouse or lover. That is, of course, if it seems to me that said client has a karmic need or desire for another romantic relationship in his or her life.

The messages most often received through the heart chakra are not heard, but felt. At this energy level we can feel joy, love, assurances, and soul-mate bonds. My widowed clients, as well as those who have lost a son or daughter to death, frequently report comforting, warming vibes in their chests. It is the kind of energy that transcends words, so it can be difficult to describe. Nevertheless, it is often accompanied by a tingling sensation at the chest level of the back. It may literally feel as though you are being hugged by a spirit or an angel.

The heart chakra is also the center of one of my least-favorite subjects: forgiveness. It's a pet peeve of mine because it has so often been my finding that those who are abusive take forgiveness as permission to be abusive again. So, I think we must be very discerning about who we grant our forgiveness. I will never recommend that anyone open his or her heart chakra indiscriminately to forgiving someone who is likely to be a repeat offender. That said, I have communicated with many of my clients' friends and relatives in Heaven who seek forgiveness every chance they get. It seems to be a prerequisite for the purification of their souls and their abilities to move on from the more purgatorial levels of Heaven into what I call "Heaven proper." It is probably, in our earthly vernacular, part of a "12-step program" of some sort.

In any case, I always view the forgiveness process as a mark of our personal power. I believe we have the right to decide, without premature urging, when and even if we will forgive a certain individual. Some earthly acts just strike me as too evil and horrendous to forgive. They, therefore, must be referred to Christ or other sacred beings who are much stronger in the forgiveness department, than we mere mortals tend to be.

When I receive a request for forgiveness from someone on the Other Side, I tell my client I will "acknowledge" the request, but not accept it. Acceptance of an apology is solely the decision of my customer, when and if he or she chooses to grant it. By the same token, the heart chakra is where we all will have to go in order to seek forgiveness for our own deeds. Many of my clients find themselves so wracked with guilt after the death of a loved one or pet that they seem unable to progress through the grief-healing process until we actively acknowledge what they feel they did to hurt the deceased individual. This ranges from deep regret that they were unable to get to a hospital or hospice deathbed by the time of a loved one's passing to the great anguish pet owners can feel about being unable to communicate to a dog or cat why they chose to have them euthanized for a fatal illness.

Because none of us is perfect, we will all seek forgiveness at some point in our lives. If the person or pet you want it from has passed away, the heart chakra is the clearinghouse for these requests. In fact, I have even heard of forgiveness being experienced in this energy center, when it was *not* requested! Sometimes we require forgiveness from Heaven, even if we don't actively acknowledge this need. Like a ship getting freed from an impeding sandbar, forgiveness can allow us to move on with our karmic journeys.

As Alexander Pope said, it is, indeed, human to err and "divine" to forgive. All I can say in conclusion is that I'm eternally grateful that Heaven reserves that right to decide which souls are salvageable and which are not, because it is far too momentous a decision to be left to us fallible humans.

Meditating on Your Solar-Plexus Chakra

Located in the upper part of the abdomen, the solar plexus is the chakra with which most Westerners are innately familiar. This fact is borne out by such commonly used phrases as "butterflies in my stomach," "I had a gut feeling," or "my stomach was tied in knots." While your solar plexus is not technically your stomach, it's the chakra we associate with it. Whenever we're nervous, afraid or just ill at ease, this is the energy center where we're likely to know it beyond a doubt.

Conversely, if we're feeling sure of our beliefs, self-confident, and more than capable of fighting the good fight, this sometimes-cowardly chakra can become a sacred warrior who strides ahead with stunning fortitude and resolve. At such times, we have the "guts" to stand up for ourselves and others, as well as to claim what is rightfully ours in this life. It makes sense, then, that the music for this chakra is any kind of march. While such music is a perfect choice for empowering yourself, I don't recommend listening to marches when seeking afterlife communications in this chakra.

Rather, you should choose music that strikes you as both comforting and healing.

In the face of grief, the solar plexus can either cave in under the weight of loss or push through it with the well-centered force of a snowplow. Thus, this energy center benefits from physical exercises which strengthen the stomach and the back, such as sit-ups and certain yoga poses. Also, be sure to eat foods which have been proven to support stomach health, such as apples and yogurt.

The psychic version of strengthening this chakra is to regularly ask it for its response to the occurrences in your life and the decisions you're making about them. The more you seek answers from your solar plexus, rather than trying to get your direction from other people, the stronger this chakra will become.

Afterlife messages received at this energy point tend to be sent by deceased children and pets. These are emotional and basic messages, not the more cerebral types you're likely to receive through the crown, brow, and throat chakras. The solar plexus is where straightforward spirits go to say simple, yet infinitely meaningful things like, "I love you" or "I'm always with you." But don't expect actual words or images at this level, because, more often than not, these afterlife messages will be conveyed as feelings and sentiments in the form of warmth or surges of energy. This is also the chakra in which clairsentience or clear-knowing is strongest. The solar plexus is a terrific judge of the accuracy of the spirit messages we receive. It can quickly tell you if the information you're getting is right or wrong. It can also confirm the identity of the soul who is communicating with you.

When meditating on the solar-plexus, light a lemon-scented candle, because the color of this chakra is yellow and its essential oils come from citrus fruits. Then, stare at the candle and imagine its warm, yellow glow moving into you at the level of your upper abdomen. When you need solace and reassurances from your loved ones in Heaven, this is where you're most likely to find them. In fact, some of my clients have told me their weeping after the death of a loved one ended when they experienced the strong, healing glow Heaven can instill in this chakra.

Meditating on Your Sacral Chakra

The sacral chakra is located two inches below your navel and two inches into your pelvic area. It's an energy center that is all about pleasure and abundance. Spirits who visit you here do so with touch and by giving you stimulating and satisfying sensations. They are almost always our deceased spouses or lovers or even romantic soul mates from past lives. My clients who are widows or widowers are always tremendously relieved when I confirm that it's perfectly normal for them to feel their passed spouse is sleeping with them or even making love to them. The deceased loved ones with whom we were most intimate naturally crave sexual connections with us and they are often eager to share the powerful spiritual aspects of lovemaking, which their newfound soul bodies bring to such unions. It is, therefore, not uncommon for such encounters to entail telepathic images of Heaven and your spouse or lover's home there. My customers have reported seeing all of the following during these spiritual-sexual encounters: ethereal colors and lights, visions of vacation spots, waterfalls, tropical locations, and even cradling, bed-like images of clouds.

According to most of the spirits I've talked to for my clients, many of the levels of Heaven are indescribably beautiful. It stands to reason, then, that our passed spouses and lovers want to share some of these surroundings with us, especially when they're experiencing the ecstasy of lovemaking.

The music of this chakra is Latin dance. Its color is orange, so scent your bed pillows with orange-blossom oil or citrus-based cologne. Or you may choose your deceased lover's brand of perfume or aftershave cologne for this purpose.

Lovemaking in Heaven always takes place between souls who are genuinely in love with one another. It's an expression of mutual trust and a means of physical and spiritual coupling which allows both parties to reach otherworldly levels and potentials never before experienced. In short, it's about the growth and expansion of the soul, creative endeavors, and a merging of energies which helps invigorate both parties involved. You should come away from these intimate encounters feeling less alone and more enlivened. Just be aware that there are predatory spirits, nonresidents of Heaven, who have been known to sexually violate the living. So, always confirm with your solar plexus and your other chakras that the soul who is attempting to merge with you is, indeed, your deceased lover or spouse.

If such an encounter becomes painful or unpleasant, or, if you're feeling inappropriately dominated or compelled to engage in behavior with which you're uncomfortable, it's likely you're being visited by an unknown spirit. In that case, demand aloud that he or she leave your presence immediately and never return. Having said that, it's extremely rare for a living individual to be visited in the sacral chakra by a spirit who is not a deceased spouse, lover, or a known romantic partner.

Meditating on Your Root Chakra

Finally we come to the end of the rainbow within you: the chakra at the base of your spine. While this is not an energy center that's receptive to afterlife messages, it can serve some important purposes in the balance between the physical and the spiritual worlds. The root chakra is what anchors you to the Earth at times when you're feeling too flighty or out-of-body. Represented by the Archangel Michael, Heavenly warrior against evil, this chakra helps to keep chaotic and malicious energy out of your life. This makes it the perfect energy point at which to *start* an all-chakra mediation. Feeling grounded and protected can help you trust the spiritual encounters you have with all of your other energy points.

When meditating on the base of your spine, you may want to light a red candle, since that's the color of this level of your body. Holding a ruby, bloodstone, or hematite is helpful during such a meditation, as is taking a few whiffs of cinnamon oil or sage. Listening to drumming is also recommended. Don't focus on this chakra for more than a couple minutes, however, as its chief purpose is to bind your spirit to the Earth and material possessions, which can counter the goal of communicating with the spirit world.

Soul-Sensing Summary

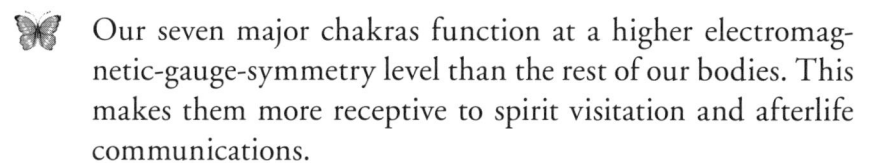

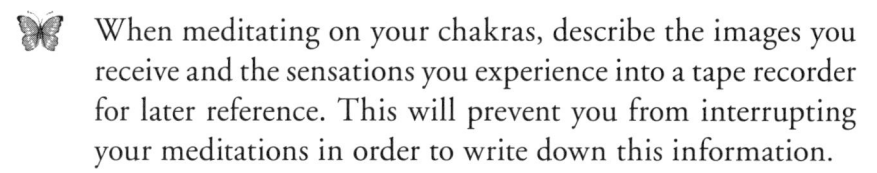

- Our seven major chakras function at a higher electromagnetic-gauge-symmetry level than the rest of our bodies. This makes them more receptive to spirit visitation and afterlife communications.

- When meditating on your chakras, describe the images you receive and the sensations you experience into a tape recorder for later reference. This will prevent you from interrupting your meditations in order to write down this information.

- The crown chakra is the most spiritually pure. It attracts truly angelic energy, highly evolved spirits, and the most learned and wise of our deceased loved ones.

- The brow chakra represents your inner vision, such as the images you see when you're dreaming in your sleep. The second type of images you may receive by strengthening your brow chakra is actual, physical glimpses of the spirits of your deceased loved ones. This usually begins with your peripheral vision and may grow stronger with time.

- The throat chakra governs both hearing and speaking. This is where you can hear messages with your "inner ear." This is also the chakra that allows your deceased loved ones to channel messages out of your mouth. The soul senses of clear-smelling and clear-tasting occur in this energy center, as well.

- The heart chakra connects you with all other souls, dead or living. It is the energy center that both grants and receives forgiveness. Afterlife messages received at this level are usually felt, rather than heard.

- Communications from deceased pets and children are most often received in the solar-plexus chakra. Feelings and sentiments experienced at this level usually take the form of warmth or surges of energy.

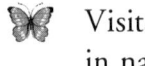

- Visits at the level of the sacral chakra are sexual or creative in nature. This is where our passed spouses, lovers (or even soul mates from past lives) can merge with us in amorous ways.

- The root chakra generally does not receive afterlife communications, but it can protect you from negative-spirit energy and invasion.

Chapter 8

Soul Sensing With Your Intuition

Not everyone is psychic, but we are all intuitive to some extent. We all get gut feelings about the people and situations in our lives. Often, intuitive information and images just pop into our minds, but we're not confident enough to believe in them, let alone to act upon them. This is because there are several stumbling blocks to understanding and trusting the spiritual messages we receive via our intuition.

Sabotaging Self-Talk

The first of these is your own self-talk. Does your inner voice say things like this? "I'm not psychic. The few times I've correctly predicted things were because I knew the personalities and circumstances involved." Or "My 'clairvoyance' was just dumb luck."

If these are the kinds of things you say to yourself, reprogram your self-talk by repeating this several times: "I'm a spiritual being living in a physical body. Because of this, I'm connected to Heaven, the spirit world, and the wisdom of my soul senses."

If your self-talk says, "How can I be sure the messages I receive are not just products of my imagination,"—redirect it by saying this to yourself: "Every afterlife message I receive has some validity, even if I don't recognize it immediately."

Validity in Every Message

We professional mediums must deal with the subjectivity of spirit messages all the time. In fact, I've learned to prefer doing sessions with two or more members of a family, rather than just one. This is because what one of them doesn't recognize or remember, another one usually will.

My most recent experience with this was when I was bringing through messages for the mother and grown sister of a young man who had committed suicide. It was a phone session during which the sister was a few minutes late in joining us. I was telling the mom that her deceased son was talking about one of his winter coats. He was emphatic that he'd been given a coat by a family member or that he'd given a coat to one of them. His mother, however, had no knowledge or memory of this. Nevertheless, my faith in the medium process allowed me to hear her son's conviction about this and know, beyond a doubt, that it was a valid message.

Once the deceased's sister came on the phone line, I repeated the message to her, and she sheepishly confessed to her mother and me that she had recently taken one of her dead brother's coats from the front closet of her parents' home. "I've been wearing it," she explained, "because it has his scent on it and that helps me not to miss him as much."

Now, had I been a beginner at bringing through afterlife messages, I would probably have let the coat message go, fearing I'd strike out with the sister, as I had with the mom. Because I know that almost every message is legitimate, however, this young man's soul was able to confirm for his sister that he had seen what she did and he was touched enough by it to acknowledge it to her.

You owe it to yourself and your deceased loved one to bring the same kind of faith to your afterlife-communication efforts. Remember that almost every message, image, or sign you receive from the Other Side is valid, especially if it's repeated or recurrent.

Even if you don't remember or recognize it, tell it to others who knew your passed loved one and see if any of them do.

Internal Gauges

The second hurdle you may face in using your intuition to bring through afterlife messages is being too "outer directed." This means depending too much on other people's opinions, rather than turning inward for a private sense of what is correct and accurate for you personally. When you receive what you think is a message or sign from a passed loved one, close your eyes and concentrate on your solar-plexus chakra (your upper abdomen). Quietly repeat to yourself the message you received or the sign you perceived. Then fall silent for several seconds and notice what you feel at this level of your body. If you experience a sensation of warmth or feel tingles anywhere on your torso, the message is genuinely from the Other Side.

If you wish, you can use this same "gut-check" method to get more specifics about the message you received. For instance, use it to determine who sent it and why. Remember, though, that it's always best to make your inquiries in the form of yes-or-no questions. Your solar plexus or torso will not respond, if the answer is no. If the answer is yes, however, you'll feel the aforementioned warmth or tingles.

Another way to get a quick yes-or-no answer is to shut your eyes and imagine a sign that reads "Yes" in front of your right eyeball and a sign that reads "No" in front of your left. The spirit who is trying to communicate with you will instantly choose one or the other. This should happen so quickly that you will not have a chance to consciously choose one eye or the other on your own.

Both of these methods of confirming messages help strengthen your abilities to be intuitive, because they depend upon your physical senses, as well as your soul senses. Unlike using external tools, such as tarot cards, to receive and confirm afterlife messages, these two methods directly contribute to your soul-sensery development.

Just a Coincidence?

Another hurdle to receiving and recognizing afterlife messages through intuition is the "it's-just-a-coincidence" mindset. This spiritual obstruction assigns almost every occurrence to chance or imagination. When we're looking at our intuitive messages and experiences through this filter, we often miss or shrug off what is significant, making it that much harder for our deceased loved ones to get their messages across to us. Indeed, so-called "coincidences" are actually an integral part of the language of the dead. Admittedly, there are random coincidences and there are *meaningful* coincidences, and we must learn to discern which is which. When it comes to afterlife communications, meaningful coincidences are always encoded with meaning that is pertinent to you and your deceased loved one. They establish or recount an unmistakable connection between you and the person or pet whom you've lost to death.

Synchronicities

Swiss psychiatrist Carl Jung wrote extensively about meaningful coincidences, ultimately naming them "synchronicities." He defined them as two or more events that are unlikely to occur together or close to each other in space and time, but, nevertheless, do. Although they are not causally related, they come together in a meaningful manner. We professional mediums know that true synchronicities are integral to the language of the afterlife. To dismiss them as mere happenstance is to ignore some of the most meaningful interplay our deceased loved ones' souls can have with our spirits. My good friends Trish and Rob MacGregor wrote a recently published, must-read book on the subject of attracting such communications: *The 7 Secrets of Synchronicity: Your Guide to Finding Meaning in Signs Big and Small*. In it they offer lots of exercises for recognizing coincidences in our day-to-day lives. In fact, while writing their book, it became apparent to them that synchronicities so often apply to the spirit world that their in-the-works sequel will deal entirely with that subject.

In over 18 years of doing medium work for others, my clients have shared with me so many instances of synchronicities with their deceased loved ones that I cannot possibly write them all off as random occurrences. Just read a couple of the accounts they've shared with me below and you'll understand what I mean.

A few weeks after my client Sally's husband died, some friends took her out boating on the Fourth of July. When their yacht was pulling out of the marina, Sally spotted a 1960s cabin cruiser that had belonged to her husband five years earlier! She and her friends looked it over to make sure it was the same boat: a shiny wooden Chris-Craft with dark-red seat covers and a cabin big enough to sleep two. The clincher, however, was what Sally's husband had painted on the stern of the boat. It read "Sally Sue"— the affectionate name he'd given the vessel decades earlier.

Just a coincidence? I hardly think so. In fact, Sally's husband sold the boat to a man who lived on a lake over three hundred miles away from where Sally and her friends were spending Independence Day. So, the odds of it turning up in Sally's part of town were not high. Thus, with this well-engineered synchronicity, Sally's husband told her that his soul was still alive and able to reach out to her in significant ways.

Naming Names

Another synchronicity I hear about quite often from my clients has to do with the names of those who have passed. A case in point happened to a customer I'll call Lee. Her mother died a few years ago of cancer, and Lee and her sister, Larisse, were at their mom's hospital deathbed when she passed. Lee told me she felt inconsolable once a doctor came into the room to confirm her mother was dead. Yet, seconds later, when a nurse entered to assist him, Lee was so surprised by what she saw that her sobs caught in her throat. The first name on this nurse's badge was "Sonia." Oddly enough, Lee's mother was also named Sonia. Lee knew instantly that this synchronicity was a message from her mom's spirit and that it was meant to console her daughters. However, Lee's sister, Larisse, was not convinced that this coincidence was due to anything more than chance.

Two days later though, Larisse became a believer as well. She and Lee were at the local mortuary, finalizing the arrangements for their mother's burial with a funeral director. A receptionist entered the room to give the director a phone message, the director asked her to bring two of the mortuary's business cards into his office and give them to Lee and Larisse so they would have all the phone numbers they needed for any last-minute concerns. When the receptionist returned with the cards seconds later, Larisse gasped. The cards bore the director's last name, which he had not given when he'd introduced himself to the two women. It was Sonia! Both daughters were in agreement that Sonia was just too uncommon a name for this second "coincidence" to be anything except a message from their mother's soul.

How Psychic Are You?

Because we don't address the subject of death much in Western culture, we are much less likely to do the spiritual exercises necessary for communicating with the dead. Most of us know the importance of physical development through workouts and intellectual development through reading and learning. If, however, you ask people what they've done lately to contribute to their psychic or soul development, you're likely to get a blank look. Be that as it may, in order to build connections with our deceased loved ones, we must add some easy-to-do psychic exercises to our day-to-day lives. In preparing a quick psychic quiz for this book, I took several things into consideration:

1. What could I offer you that is more interesting than the classic, academic shape-in-a-box test? (You know, the one where you indicate which of these shapes a test-controller or computer software has chosen: a square, a circle, a triangle, or a star.) Believe me, that gets old in a hurry.

2. How could I preserve the multiple-choice format of the shape-in-the-box quiz?

3. What could I give you to test your intuitive abilities without involving one of your friends or relatives in the process? (Most psychic tests require having another party physically place objects in a bag for you to guess at. Or having someone else choose magazine photos for you to try to mentally picture. Or even having another party hide a coin somewhere for you to find.)

The following multiple-choice questions will help you assess your ability to perceive information that you cannot possibly know. This exercise will assist you in determining how well you gather information put forth by my soul, and that's fitting, since soul communication is what you're doing when you receive messages from the spirit of your passed loved one.

Before you take the quiz, let me offer a couple tips that will help keep you out of your deductive left brain during this exercise. To begin with, *first impressions are usually your best bet* when it comes to psychic communications. Secondly, don't just choose the longest answer, believing it to be correct. I'm onto that college-quiz-taking trick, so I've been careful not to show my hand to you with that. Please don't just guess at these questions. Instead, pay attention to the answer your eyes are most drawn to; then ask your intuition to confirm or reject it for you.

Lastly, relax and have fun with this exercise. This will help you move into your intuitive right brain as you answer the questions.

Here goes. Just circle the answer that immediately strikes you as correct.

1. What is my (Janice Carlson's) favorite color?
    Periwinkle
    Hot pink
    Mustard yellow

2. Which of these is my (Janice Carlson's) favorite number between 1 and 10?
    7
    10
    4

3. Which of these flowers do I (Janice Carlson) like best?
    Tulip
    Daisy
    Rose

4. Which meal do I (Janice Carlson) like best?
    Breakfast
    Lunch
    Supper

5. Which of these is my (Janice Carlson's) favorite season?
    Spring
    Summer
    Autumn

To see how you scored, please go to the answers listed at the end of this chapter.

How did you do? If you got two or more right, be encouraged. You're probably much more intuitive than most people. Even if you did poorly on this quiz, however, your intuitive abilities will improve, because I'm going to give you some easy psychic-development exercises to add to your everyday life.

Close Does Count

When I first tried this quiz out on a few of my professional associates and friends, I did not present it to them as multiple-choice questions. I just asked, "What's my favorite color?" and, invariably, their answer was "blue." This is interesting, because the definition of periwinkle is blue-violet. The reason why this is significant is because *close counts in psychic work*. I used to believe the old adage, "Close only counts in horseshoes." But this simply isn't true when it comes to mediumship. When you enter the world of spiritual communications, images, connections, and even vague impressions all count as legitimate forms of information transfer. For instance, one of my friends, a non-gardener, wasn't sure what a tulip looks like. Instead, she eliminated the label barrier with this question and just sketched an image of a blossom that she thought she was receiving from my mind. She drew a flower with rounded, concentric petals. It was much more like a rose than a daisy or a tulip. This was a very useful exercise, since spirits sometimes resort to having us draw symbols, when words are getting in the way of their meanings. What's more, in nearly two decades of doing medium work for others, I've yet to encounter a spirit who presented information in multiple-choice form!

So, even though standard psychic tests employ multiple-choice questions, it's usually the making-connections portion of such communications that's most significant with afterlife messages, and close *does* count. When questions are presented to us in multiple-choice form, we become more aware that there's a correct answer to the question and any other choice is wrong. With this mindset we naturally become attached to being right, rather than listening to our intuition and soul senses to answer the question. This attachment to being right or, conversely, the fear of being wrong, works to shut down our right-brain, soul-sensing functions. So, with that said, let's try a similar set of questions and see how you do without the restrictions of the multiple-choice format.

1. What's Janice Carlson's favorite type of wild bird?

(Describe any colors, images, or other details that come to your mind.)

2. What's Janice Carlson's favorite type of music? (i.e. Rhythm & Blues)

(Jot down any descriptions of sound, images, or other details that come to you.)

3. What's Janice Carlson's favorite musical instrument?

(Describe any shapes, textures, sounds, or images that come to your mind.)

4. What's Janice Carlson's favorite type of ethnic food?

(Jot down any aromas, flavors, colors, shapes, textures, or images that come to you.)

5. What's Janice Carlson's favorite type of gemstone?

(Describe any colors, shapes, textures, or images that come to your mind.)

Check your responses against the answers listed at the *end* of the Soul-Sensing Summary section of this chapter.

How did you do? My guess is you did better than or about the same as on the first quiz. This is amazing, when you consider that you had a 1-in-3 chance of guessing the right answers in the first exercise! Remember, too, that close counts. Any colors and images you received that correlated with my answers are significant. For instance, rather than seeing an emerald as my favorite gemstone, one of my friends chose a peridot, which is also a green stone. I think that's pretty darn close, given the vast spectrum of colored precious stones from which she had to choose.

Others of my volunteer test-takers simply saw a string instrument as my favorite. Some of them even added "with a round bottom." Again, as any professional medium will tell you, *close counts* when it comes to using your intuition to receive afterlife messages. Overall, I found myself very surprised at how intuitive my self-professed "not-psychic" volunteers proved to be.

Strengthening Your Psychic Abilities

Now, how can you start strengthening your intuition on a regular basis—that is, without enlisting the help of often-too-busy friends and family? Begin by taking advantage of these easy daily opportunities:

1. Predict who is calling you before you answer your phone.

2. Predict how many people will attend an upcoming meeting, family gathering, or social event to which you've been invited.

3. If you work in or frequently visit a building with elevators, predict which floors it will stop on, while you're waiting to board it.

4. Watch game shows and predict the answers to the questions (assuming you don't consciously know them).

5. Secretly predict which colors your coworkers will be wearing tomorrow.

6. Predict which breed of dog you'll see next on TV, in a passing car, or while you're out walking.

7. Predict final scores in sporting events.

All of these exercises take just seconds out of your day. This should leave you a minute here and there to write your answers in a daily planner and to keep track of your progress at strengthening your psychic abilities.

An Even Better Score

Before moving on to the next chapter and discovering which of the communication tools work best for you and your deceased loved one, spend several days using the seven psychic exercises I've just listed. Then take this last psychic quiz to see how much your abilities have improved.

1. How old was Janice Carlson when braces were put on her teeth?

2. What color was Janice Carlson's first car?

3. Which food does Janice Carlson hate? (Describe aromas, flavors, colors, shapes, textures, or images that come to you.)

4. What color was Janice Carlson's first pet?

5. What color was Janice Carlson's second pet?

6. What was Janice Carlson costumed as the first time she went trick-or-treating on Halloween? (Jot down any colors, shapes, or images, that come to your mind.)

Please see the answers at the end of Chapter 9. If you've been regularly testing your intuitive abilities in your day-to-day life, I'm willing to bet your score got higher. If so, ask some of your non-judgmental friends or relatives to let you psychically "read" them. See if you can tell them some of the specifics of their daily lives in the past couple weeks. You might, for example, tell them any information you receive intuitively about what they've recently eaten, purchased, read, or written. Again, you will probably be surprised by how many correct psychic details you can gather about them. It is precisely this type of interpersonal intuitive exchange that best prepares you for communication with your dead loved ones.

Once you've tested your intuition to the point of considerable improvement, it's time to employ some of the tools of the trade, which are featured in the next chapter. Not all mediums use these implements, but I will confess that they sure make afterlife communications easier. This is especially true after I've spent several nonstop hours doing psychic and medium readings at a metaphysical fair.

Not only do the resources in Chapter 9 make afterlife messaging easier, they also offer your deceased loved one or pet a broader range of ways to access your soul senses. Just as we, the living, have individual strengths and preferences in our communication methods, so do the souls in Heaven. So, if you find that one of these tools doesn't work for you, move on to another.

(Answers to first psychic quiz: **1.** Periwinkle, **2.** Four, **3.** Rose, **4.** Lunch, **5.** Autumn)

Soul-Sensing Summary

- Everyone is intuitive to some extent.
- Your negative self-talk is the biggest blocker of the psychic messages and images you receive.
- Stop dismissing the intuitive messages you receive as being nothing more than coincidences, dumb luck, or imaginings.
- Almost every afterlife message you receive has some validity—even if you don't recognize it immediately.
- If you can't identify or recall what a specific afterlife message refers to, one of your friends or family members who knew your passed loved one probably can.
- If an afterlife message is repeated to you or recurrent in your mind, your deceased loved one is determined to have you acknowledge it.
- Don't depend on other people's opinions or beliefs when deciding on the validity of an intuitive or afterlife message. Judge the message using your solar-plexus chakra.
- So-called "coincidences" and synchronicities are an integral part of the language of the dead. You must, however, learn to differentiate between random coincidences and *meaningful* ones.
- When it comes to receiving information psychically, first impressions are most often correct.
- Multiple-choice tests of psychic ability appear to limit the right-brain's receptivity.

There are several psychic exercises you can do in your day-to-day life to strengthen both your intuition and your ability to receive afterlife messages.

(Answers to second psychic quiz: **1.** Cardinal, **2.** Bluegrass, **3.** Banjo, **4.** Mexican, **5.** Emerald)

Chapter 9

Afterlife-Communication Tools and How to Use Them

One of the blind spots inherent in being a longtime practitioner of anything is that you assume it will come easily for everyone else. Using a tarot deck for afterlife communications is like rolling off a log for me. But, then again, I've been reading tarot cards for over 20 years. All this to say that you will probably be best off test-driving the tools detailed in this chapter for psychic work, before attempting to use them for afterlife communications.

I recommend you start with a few questions about recent events in your life, to see if the answers you receive relate to what's actually going on with you. This is something I do for people seeking a psychic reading from me for the first time. I offer them a piece or two of information about their lives at present, and, if what I tell them is correct, odds are very good I'll be the right psychic for predicting their futures.

So, with each of the tools I'm about to present to you, start with questions about *your* past or present. These should be queries to which you definitely know the answers, and then you can see if one method resonates more for you than the others. Afterlife communications can be obscure and hard to decipher, so it's best to use a tool with which you have built up a comfort level.

I should also note here that all of the communication devices I'll present in this chapter can be consecrated and protected by saying a prayer while holding them. Simply request of Heaven that they be used only for good and never for evil.

Be Prepared For the Truth

When you start using tools for afterlife communications, the messages you receive become more specific than the ones you get through your chakras and intuition. So, bear in mind that, while your deceased loved one no longer experiences physical pain or need, he or she does still possess emotions—some of them negative. Our passed loved ones can still feel worried, angry, and sad. But it's been my finding that these emotions are much more related to the circumstances of the living than anything that's happening in the afterlife. Based on all I've heard about Heaven from the dead, it's a place where there is no physical pain, no addiction, no hunger or thirst, and no crime. All of that would make it, by definition, a much better place to be than on earth. If your loved one misses you, however, he or she may express some sadness. If your passed relative or friend thinks the life path you're on is perilous or ill-advised, she may convey concern and sometimes even anger. If your loved one got to Heaven and discovered his karmic "report card" was not up to par, he may let you know there's a lot of work ahead in the afterlife to improve those grades. Naturally, this isn't news that evokes happiness. There is, however, always a measure of relief reflected in the communications of such an individual, because he is being given a chance for redemption from the Other Side, rather than being sent back to Earth for a much more difficult remedial effort. All this to say you should expect your deceased loved one to express negative emotions from time to time. Without them, how could any of our souls possibly learn and improve?

Pendulums

While pendulums allow only four answers ("yes," "no," "maybe," or "I don't know") they are ideal for your initial contact with a deceased loved one. Part of what makes pendulums perfect for this is that you probably already own one or can assemble one using a string or thin chain with a key or other small object dangling from it.

Secondly, lightweight pendulums are subatomic-matter friendly. That is to say, the dead rarely, if ever, move anything heavy; so light items, like small, hanging objects are perfect for them. I have found that a pendulum weighing one-half of an ounce (including its chain or string) is just right. If it weighs .7 ounces or more, it will be less responsive to the influences of the dead.

To prepare for pendulum use:

1. Write out your questions and messages for your passed loved one or friend, so you're ready to interact promptly.

2. Remember to *begin with questions that establish the identity of the spirit with whom you wish to communicate.*

For instance, you might ask, "Dad, are you making this pendulum swing?" Then the spirit can give you an affirmative or negative reply.

You can get further confirmation of a spirit's identity by moving on to more complicated "yes/no" questions. These should be queries to which you're sure only a specific dead loved one will know the answers. For instance, a widow might ask her passed husband, "Did we consider naming our first son 'Oliver?'" Or "Did we kiss on our first date?"

Here is how to use a pendulum for afterlife communications:

1. Prop an elbow on a level, solid surface, like a table or desk.

2. Using the hand propped over the solid surface, hold the pendulum's chain between your forefinger and thumb.

3. Let the chain and pendulum dangle freely, where they won't bump into anything when they start to swing.

4. Ask your yes/no questions out loud and hold the chain as still as possible.

5. If the pendulum begins to swing towards you, then away from you, like the nodding of a head, the spirit is answering "yes" to your inquiry.

6. If the pendulum starts to swing side to side, like the shaking of a head, it's saying "no."

7. If it moves in a circular or diagonal motion, this can be interpreted as "maybe" or "I don't know."

8. Please note that it can take several seconds for your pendulum to switch directions between questions, so give it some time to show a definitive new swing.

If you wish to send messages, rather than just receiving them during this session, speak aloud, then ask if your love one heard and understood you. You may also ask for a positive or negative response to your message. Once again, positive is a back-and-forth swing. Negative is a side-to-side swing. If the spirit is undecided or confused by what you said, your pendulum will move in a circular or diagonal manner. Should this happen, ask if your loved one is unsure of what you meant. You might need to rephrase your question or statement. We can't always count on those in the afterlife to be able to read our thoughts. So, the more clear and precise you can be in stating your messages aloud to them, the better.

Afterlife-Communication Tools and How to Use Them

Playing Cards

When you feel that it's time to move beyond asking yes/no questions, you can avoid spending money on intuitive tools by using a deck of ordinary playing cards. The suits and symbols on them will start the process of feeding you information from the Other Side.

Later in this chapter, I will explain how to bring through afterlife messages by using tarot cards. But, for now, let's see how well you do with an everyday pack of 52. Because some people feel uncomfortable with the tarot deck, believing centuries of bad press about them, you may find yourself more at ease with familiar playing cards. Since today's "ordinary" cards are believed to be the abridged descendants of medieval tarot decks, they hold a lot of hidden meanings, which I'll explain to you shortly. In the meantime, follow these steps:

1. Do *not* remove the joker cards from your deck. If drawn, a joker sometimes indicates that your loved one is teasing you. When drawn in conjunction with applicable cards, your passed friend or relative may be reminiscing about a funny experience you both shared. In short, the jokers can help you confirm your loved one's identity by enabling you to gauge his or her sense of humor.

As with the Fool card in the tarot deck, jokers can also represent the spirit of God linking with the souls of humans. It can symbolize the coming of divine intervention, as well as something as simple as dumb luck. In addition, it's a way for the dead to say to us, "Let go and let God."

I should also note here that jacks are the same as pages or knights in the tarot deck. This means they symbolize someone coming to your aid. They can be your deceased love one's way of assuring you he or she is protecting and defending you in your day-to-day life.

2. Write down the questions you wish to ask your passed loved one.

3. Shuffle your playing cards three times, while concentrating on a photo or mental image of him or her.

4. Keeping the cards facedown, fan them out in front of you in a semi-circular formation.

Ready to start getting answers? Here are some of the hidden meanings in the cards:

Clubs

If you pull a card in the suit of clubs, your loved one is referring to ideas, thoughts, ambitions, or growth. This is a spiritual suit, because it alludes to what has yet to manifest itself in the physical world or what has not yet fully developed. Often a spirit who causes you to draw a club is reminding you of your innate talents and your ability to attract to yourself the things and opportunities you need or want.

Clubs are also about work, including physical labor and our daily jobs or careers—as well as those of the passed soul with whom you're communicating. A great example of this meaning of a club happened during a medium reading I did for a widowed client of mine. I had never used regular playing cards for medium or psychic work, so I thought I should give it a try.

Before the phone session began, I got the sense that this widow's passed husband was concerned about her safety during the current tornado season. The card he moved me to choose was the ten of clubs. This indicated that he was talking about a place he had labored to build. Knowing that the lowest level of a house is the safest place to go during a tornado warning, I asked his wife if her husband had personally finished off the basement of their house. She confirmed he had. But she admitted she still wasn't sure which part of the basement she should go to if there were a tornado. "The bathroom, maybe?" she guessed.

I pulled another card for clarification. Again, it was a high-numbered club, indicating that a great deal of work was done there. "No," I replied. "He's talking about a particular place within your basement where a lot of work was done."

"His workshop, then," she concluded. "It's opposite the walk-out side of the basement. It's made of cement-block walls on three sides and it has no windows."

Bingo! With just two playing cards, her late husband had conveyed the safest place for her and her dog to take cover during what had already proven to be an unusually deadly tornado season.

Hearts

Now it's time to move on to a suit with a meaning that is much more evident: hearts. Shaped like the hearts you would see on Valentine's Day cards, they can simply be your deceased loved one's way of saying, "I love you," especially if you draw several of them during a single communication session. I should stress, however, that the suit of hearts represents all other emotions as well. So, to fully understand which sentiment your deceased loved one is referring to, you should consider buying a copy of Nancy Garen's handbook, *Tarot Made Easy*. It's the most comprehensive tarot guide I've found, and it has been readily available in bookstores since it was first published in 1989.

Hearts are the same as the suit of cups in the tarot deck. So, by looking up the numbers of the hearts you draw within the cups section of Nancy's book, you'll get the complete meanings of the playing cards you pick. If, for instance, you pull the three of hearts, simply turn to the three of cups in Garen's book, and the

"Focus" heading will tell you that your deceased loved one is concerned about how well you're taking care of yourself, particularly spiritually and socially.

This card is pulled a lot by widows and widowers who have become too reclusive in their grief. The three of hearts (or cups) literally says, "You're not taking care of your needs." So, if you draw this card, take a personal inventory. Ask yourself: "Am I eating well? Am I spending enough time out with people? Am I going to church regularly or otherwise meeting my spiritual needs?" And, if you have a pet, this card could also be a reminder to take good care of him or her.

Our deceased loved ones seem to see almost everything we do and don't do. So, they're in a unique position to let us know when our lives are out of balance and need some adjustments.

Spades

Spades are the equivalent of the suit of swords in the tarot deck. They represent action and struggles, as well as legal matters and those in positions of authority. When you pull a spade, your dead friend or relative is probably telling you events in your life are about to accelerate. He or she may be acknowledging a current conflict in your life and letting you know roughly when or how it will be resolved. A spade can also be the deceased's way of assuring you that someone is about to come to your defense.

Again, to fully interpret what a particular spade is meant to convey, refer to the number of that card in the swords section of *Tarot Made Easy*. For example, if you draw the seven of spades, read the headings of the seven of swords. There you will see that your passed loved one is probably warning you that someone in the world of the living is trying to pull a fast one on you. (Double-check any business contracts and transactions.) Another possibility is that an illness may be sneaking up on you, so it might be time to have a medical checkup, if you haven't had one for a while. This is the general focus of this card. However, assuming you asked your loved one's soul a question before you pulled it, you should look through all of Nancy Garen's headings for the seven of swords and find the one that most closely fits the subject of your question. For instance, if you asked your passed loved one for business advice, you should read the "Work/Career," "Special Guidance," and the "Best Course of Action" sections for this card.

Diamonds

Lastly, we come to the suit of diamonds. Obvious symbols of wealth, diamonds speak primarily about money and prosperity. They can also represent manifestation of spirit into physical form, as well as evidence of life after death. So, if you were to ask your deceased loved one if he or she caused a physical sign of visitation which you observed, a diamond would confirm his/her responsibility for it.

Of all four suits, diamonds are the most likely to tell you about the details of your loved one's life in Heaven. This is because diamonds (or pentacles in the tarot deck) represent one's "just deserts" or what we earn in life, as well as in death. Again, *you must consider the meaning of any card you draw in relation to the specific question you asked before drawing it.*

It's a rare diamond that speaks of bad news. As you'll see in *Tarot Made Easy,* the only diamonds that convey less-than-happy messages are the two or five cards of this suit. The two of diamonds is primarily about ups and downs with money and undertakings, business problems and burdensome schedules. It's a card that says your passed loved one is aware of the difficulties you're having and he is trying to help from the Other Side.

The five of diamonds speaks of unpleasant situations regarding business or romance. This card also indicates external pressures in your life that are building to a breaking point. If you draw this diamond, your passed loved one is trying to tell you she understands and sympathizes with the hardships you're experiencing, and healing energy is being sent to you from Heaven. Again, however, compare the applicable Nancy Garen headings to the question you asked before you drew said card.

Angel Cards

The number of cards in an angel deck can vary. I've seen decks with 44 cards, as well as 52. Of the thousands of angels mentioned in religious traditions, the creators of these cards usually choose to depict angels specifically known for their positive energies. The angel-card deck and book I own was created by Christine Astell.

Although these cards are meant to give general guidance from some very high-ranking citizens of Heaven, some people do use them for afterlife communications, because they seem a natural match for it and they exude an unmistakably sacred energy. While they're beautiful and inspiring, I personally find angel cards too visually limited for truly effective medium work. Simply put, there just aren't enough beings and objects pictured on them to give me a full enough range of message possibilities. So, I've found them a little like playing a piano that's missing keys. What's more, these cards are intended to give you feedback from a specific angel, not from the spirit of your deceased loved one, so you may feel too much like you're trying to talk to your passed friend or family member through a third party who's steering the conversation in unrelated directions. If, however, you're comfortable with an angel deck and you feel protected from any malevolent spirits by the pictures on them, they might be the right match for you.

The What's-Next Method

I had to invent the above name for this method, because, even though it's the communication tool most often used by our dead loved ones, I've never run across a formal title for it. Named or not, it's fast, simple, and free of charge. All you have to do is shut your eyes and ask your passed relative or friend a question. Then, open your eyes and the first object you spot should provide you with an answer to the question you asked.

This method can be broadened to include what you hear or read next. Perhaps a song that held special meaning for the deceased will be the next to play on your iPod® or MP3® player. Maybe the first words you hear from someone, including TV or radio personalities, will be a channeled message from Heaven. Or it could be that the next word or sentence you read in an email, newspaper, or book will give you the answer you're seeking.

A practice called stichomancy focuses completely on written communications, encouraging you to find your answer by randomly opening a dictionary, an encyclopedia, poetry book, or any other volume and focusing on the first word or phrase your eyes light upon. Even if the answer you receive with the What's-Next method doesn't make sense to you, write it down in your afterlife-communications journal. It might click for you after you've had some time to ponder it.

Runes

Runes are an ancient set of letters from an alphabet which was used in Northern Europe in the first century A.D. You can buy a set of them at most large bookstores, along with a cloth pouch for their storage and a little booklet explaining their meanings. I bought mine for about $8.00 from a local chain bookstore, so they are usually not a budget-straining investment. The twenty-four rune symbols are printed on small glass, plastic, or stone disks, so it's a little like procuring a bag of lightweight marbles.

If you are of European descent, you may feel an immediate affinity for the runes. This could be more genetic than you realize, since these symbols were used for centuries by a wide range of people, from Scandinavia to Germany and England to Iceland. Contrary to popular belief, however, runes were not used for telling the future. The Germanic tribes who created them did not believe that the future was set in stone and unchangeable. Rather, they had their rune masters cast or toss these symbols like sets of dice—in an effort to heal the sick or injured or to ward off evil spirits. Thus, runes were not so much used by our ancestors as communication devices, as they were magical symbols. Runes are, even today, thought to be quite potent. Some present-day shamans would advise you to take great care with them, storing them in a safe place where others cannot tamper with or damage them. It is also not advisable to write down the symbols they bear, when taking notes during a runes session. Rather, you should write the name associated with that symbol.

Runes are said to be particularly effective for determining where you are along your current life course and where you are likely to end up if you stay on that path. So, you may want to start by gently shaking the runes around in their bag. Then take three of them from their pouch and set them out before you on a flat surface. (A rune kit often includes a silky cloth onto which the runes should be placed.) Reading them from *right to left,* the first stone represents your past, the second your present, and the third is your likely future—again, provided you stay on the life route you're on currently.

One afterlife-communication exercise you may want to try with runes is gathering insight into your deceased's current life in Heaven. Repeat the same three-disk draw explained above, but, this time, be aware that the first stone will tell you how your loved one's life was on Earth (a great piece of identifying information). The second symbol will tell you how that relative or friend is doing in Heaven at present, and a third will indicate whether he or she is going to reincarnate to the Earth or remain in the afterlife.

To sum up, runes can help you obtain guidance from your deceased loved one and determine how he or she is doing in Heaven. They can even enable you to receive information about reincarnation, both yours and your dead relative's or friend's. In my opinion, however, nothing offers the range of communication possibilities the next tool does.

Tarot Cards

While the exact origin of tarot cards is unknown, it's commonly believed they were developed by the ancient Egyptians. Today, there are so many styles of tarot decks to choose from that most new card readers just shop around until they find a deck that's visually pleasing to them or with which they otherwise resonate. Being the practical sort, I chose the utilitarian Rider Waite deck, when I started reading cards over two decades ago, and I've never looked back. They're the cards referenced in Nancy Garen's *Tarot Made Easy,* and "easy" sounded just fine to me. What's more, the Rider Waite deck provides a large range of images on each card. This will help your deceased loved one convey just about any message he or she wishes.

No matter which tarot deck you choose, however, all of them have some characteristics in common. In addition to the 52 ace-through-king cards in four suits, like regular playing cards, there should be 22 major-arcana cards (including the Fool, which is similar to the joker in a regular playing-card deck).

The major arcana cards represent the most significant issues in life, as opposed to day-to-day occurrences, so their meanings overpower those depicted in the rest of the deck. The major arcana cards are listed in the upcoming pages, along with what I've found to be the most common afterlife messages each conveys. However, tarot cards hold so many meanings that you should also refer to Nancy Garen's book to find the interpretations that best suit the questions you ask your dead loved one. The meaning intended may not line up exactly with the interpretations in any tarot guide. So, you might find that a "gut check" in your solar plexus chakra can give you final confirmation.

1. **The Magician** – As this name indicates, something magically positive is coming your way. This card is the one I most often associate with the miraculous abilities of angels, Christ, and God. The Magician can sometimes be your loved one's way of confirming he or she is in such sacred company in Heaven.

2. **The High Priestess** – This card can simply indicate that you're talking to a loved one who was a powerful female in your life, such as your mother, grandmother, an aunt, an older sister, a female boss, or the like. There was a Holy or sacred quality to her.

3. **The Empress** – This card may signify that you're speaking to a powerful female on the Other Side. Usually she is a relative of yours, but she could also have been someone who taught you about your own feminine side. She may have helped you with your wardrobe, makeup, or other decisions having to do with femaleness or even pregnancy. If you are a man, this person may have taught you to value and respect women.

   This card can also mean you're speaking to a deceased friend or relative who was a big lover and defender of nature and mother Earth.

4. **The Emperor** – As with the Empress, this card may identify the party you're speaking with as being a male relative of yours, one who got you in touch with your masculine side. This was a role model for leadership. It may have been someone who demonstrated or believed that one's success in life should be physically evident in the form of money, belongings, and/or prestige.

5. **The Hierophant** – This card sometimes indicates you are communicating with a parent who was widowed or divorced and probably married at least twice while on earth. If this person had more than one child, every effort was made to

treat each equally. This parent figure commanded great familial respect.

6. **The Lovers** – This card can say that you're speaking to someone who was your lover or spouse. If drawn while you're sure you're talking to another spirit, this card may mean the dead lover or spouse of the soul you're talking to has just joined your conversation.

7. **The Chariot** – This card often says your deceased loved one knows you're in the process of making an important decision and he or she is trying to help you see which choice is best for you.

8. **Strength** – This card usually says your passed loved one is aware you're experiencing a difficult phase of your life and he or she is trying to give you the strength to get through it. This spirit may also be acknowledging your strength of character, particularly in regard to family difficulties rooted in the past.

9. **The Hermit** – This card reveals that your dead loved one has seen you in solitude a lot lately. It may be his or her way of acknowledging that you've needed time alone in order to grieve or heal. It's also a way for the dead to say, "It's always darkest before the dawn," and a happier phase of your life is just around the corner. The Hermit could even be telling you that you've hidden from the world long enough.

10. **The Wheel of Fortune** – This card can mean many things, but, in the context of afterlife communications, it usually indicates that the relative or friend you're talking to was well-read or well-educated. This spirit could also be saying you should use wisdom or how-to-book advice in making high-risk decisions.

11. **Justice** – This card may be your dead loved one's way of talking about karma: yours or the deceased's. You'll typically draw this card when your passed friend or relative has some negative behavior to make amends for, such as that which arose from anger or addiction.

12. **The Hanged Man** – Taking this card at face value, it can indicate the deceased person you've contacted committed suicide or, to some degree, chose to die through reckless, drunken, or drug-addled behavior.

    If drawn later in your communication session, it may simply be your loved one's way of referring to someone else who died in such a manner.

13. **Death** – Although many people believe this to be the most ominous card in the tarot deck, it speaks more of resurrection than it does of physical death. It can be your loved one's way of assuring you his or her spirit rose from the dead and is still very much alive in Heaven. Also, because of this card's references to ashes, it can simply be a confirmation that the body of the soul you're speaking to was cremated, rather than buried.

    If you've received signs of visitation from your loved one, this card can establish that he or she was the one visiting you.

14. **Temperance** – Perhaps the most angelic of the tarot deck, this card can be your friend's or relative's way of saying he or she is sending you healing energy for an illness or addiction. The Temperance card can also be him or her telling you that you need to become more in touch with the ways of Heaven and spiritual teachings. In addition, this card can be a warning to you against any kind of excess.

15. **The Devil** – While I never advocate talking to spirits who reside outside the realm of Heaven, this card can mean you're speaking with a soul in the purgatorial regions of the afterlife. This loved one may have wrestled, in life, with demons or addictions, and, therefore, still have remedial work to do on the Other Side. This could also be someone who had an unhealthy and inequitable relationship with a spouse or lover.

16. **The Tower** – This card is a warning from your dead friend or relative that some part of the current earthly order is about to come crashing down. This spirit could be cautioning you about your business or personal life or an upcoming divorce. The Tower can also serve as a monition about your local, state, or national government being shaken to its roots. Because the dead function beyond our realm of space and time, they can occasionally foretell future events. You should probably ask more questions of your loved one and draw more cards for clarification.

17. **The Star** – This is a uniquely spiritual card, because it often speaks of your future in Heaven with your loved one. It also refers to spirit visitation in your dreams. If you draw the Star, it can be a request or reminder to pay closer attention to your night dreams. Your loved one is trying to commune with you in them.

18. **The Moon** – If you have a deceased pet in your past, this card can mean he or she is popping into your reading to say hello and assure you of pet survival in Heaven.

    The Moon can also represent a passed relative or acquaintance about whom you have negative or mixed feelings. Often such a spirit is trying to apologize to you for his or her behavior while on earth. If you think this is the case, acknowledge the apology aloud—even if you're not yet ready to forgive and forget. Then ask this spirit to leave you alone, unless you wish to continue conversing with him or her.

19. **The Sun** – One of the most cheerful cards in the tarot deck, the Sun can represent a deceased loved one who was the center of your life or who felt you were the center of his or hers. The Sun tells us a lot about the nature of Heaven and your deceased's ongoing spiritual quests there. This card can also serve as an assurance that your dead relative, friend, or pet is now free of physical pain and illness.

20. **Judgment** – In my opinion, no tarot card says, "I have risen from the dead" like this one. It can simply be your friend's or relative's way of affirming there is an afterlife. It can also herald the beginning of beneficial spirit flowing through you, in order to help you heal, prosper, and experience a very positive change of consciousness.

21. **The World** – This card may very well be your loved one's way of talking about life on Earth. It's likely he or she is going to have to return to the Earth to resolve some karma or fulfill a celestial mission.

22. **The Fool** – As previously mentioned, a joker sometimes indicates that your loved one is teasing you. He or she may be reminiscing about a funny experience you both shared. It can also represent both the coming of divine intervention or dumb luck. In addition, it's a way for the dead to say, "Let go and let God."

First Impressions Count

No matter which tarot card you draw, pay close attention to the *first* object or figure that catches your eye on it. This is very often central to what your passed loved one wishes to say to you.

Sample Tarot-Communication Session

As a professional medium, I rarely need to use tarot cards in order to communicate with the dead. As a soul senser, however, you may find them invaluable in your efforts to receive afterlife messages. To help show you how to use them more fully, I enlisted the help of a friend of mine, who died of lung cancer several years ago. I mentioned her earlier in this book, when I was telling you about the signs of visitation. Helen Bartlett was a beautiful woman who I met in the late 1980s. She lived here in Minnesota for a year or so; then she moved to Arizona. Nevertheless, we continued our friendship long-distance for the next fifteen years. I was unaware of her fatal illness, even though I had warned her many times to stop smoking.

When her daughter, Erica, phoned to inform me of Helen's death, she claimed her mom was so convinced that a renowned Mexican healer could cure her cancer that Helen did not acknowledge the terminal nature of her condition until a day or so before her death. (Don't get me wrong: I'm a big believer in shamanic healings. The healer Helen chose, however, was so in-demand that she did not get an appointment with him, until her disease was too advanced for anyone to save her life.) Because of this, Helen and I never got a chance for any kind of closure. So, I made a list of questions and topics for Helen to address through my tarot cards, if she was willing.

I started by asking her to identify herself. Helen was a funny, intelligent, and generous woman, and you're sure to see those personality traits as her spiritual "signature" in the cards she prompted me to choose.

> **1st card: 10 of Cups** – This card usually refers to a brunette mother and a female child who also has dark hair. This was true of Helen and her daughter, Erica.
>
> **2nd card: Nine of Cups** – The fact that I drew a second cup doesn't surprise me, since this is the suit of emotions. Helen was driven by her feelings, easily laughing or crying. As a twice-divorced mother, she did have to focus upon the things listed under Nancy Garen's "Focus" heading of this card: Career, food, and shelter. As Garen's "Desire" heading of this card indicates, however, Helen fully believed that matters always work out well for those who have faith in God and Heaven.

When I asked Helen to further identify herself by telling me about her careers in life, she switched to the suit of pentacles (or coins). This is an appropriate choice for talking about how one made money on Earth. In fact, two cards came out of my card spread, when I asked this question of Helen. When this happens, turn both of the cards face up and notice the ways in which they fine tune each other's meanings.

> **3rd card: Four of Pentacles** – Reading from left to right, this card came up first, indicating Helen started out in a career that did not pay well (secretarial work).
>
> **4th card: 10 of Pentacles** – This card is about making or inheriting a lot of money. Helen bought a dry-cleaning business when she was in her late 40s. By working very long days, she began earning six figures a year. This resulted in her being able to stop renting and buy a lovely house for herself and her daughter—complete with a huge below-ground pool in her backyard.

Satisfied that I now had my friend Helen Bartlett on the afterlife phone line, I decided to move away from "identifying" questions and onto the subject of her present life in Heaven.

5th card: Death – Helen must have been reading along as I wrote the previous section of this chapter, regarding the tarot's major-arcana cards. As I explained there, the Death card is an ideal way for a dead friend or relative to assure us his/her spirit has risen from the dead. What's more, Erica did inform me that her mother's body was cremated, in accordance with Helen's wishes, thus the Garen "Outcome" reference with this card to rising from one's own ashes.

I took a closer look at Garen's meanings of the Death card to discover what else Helen was trying to tell me about her experiences since she died. Per Garen's "Focus heading," this card speaks of a total reformation: new beginnings in lifestyle, career, and relationships. It also tells of happiness due to reuniting with friends and relatives who have been "absent." And don't we all think of our deceased loved ones as absent from our lives? This was obviously Helen's way of saying she was happy to be reunited with her brother, who died a couple years before she did—as well as her other loved ones in Heaven.

The Death card isn't just about a paradisiacal life in Heaven, however. It's "Emotional State" heading indicates that Helen was not initially happy to have died. Naturally, she found the experience of dying overwhelming—especially because she was in such a state of denial about the seriousness of her illness. This is a sentiment I hear a lot from spirits who died suddenly or at what they considered to be "before their times." Helen was only in her mid-50s when she passed away, and she left behind a much-beloved daughter and grandson.

I'm especially grateful to Helen for moving me to draw this card, because it highlights the first important point I made in this chapter: *Be prepared for the truth.* Heaven is not just everlasting joy. Its new residents often deeply miss those they've left behind on Earth, which is probably why so many of us experience signs of their visitation very soon after a loved one's death.

I had several yes/no questions I wanted to ask Helen, but, because those are best answered by a pendulum session, I decided to make a more complicated inquiry of her. I asked if she would confirm she's still in touch with me by describing anything she had recently seen me doing.

6th **card: Queen of Cups** – Nancy Garen's "Focus" heading for this card mentions "books, research, and study," as well as getting "ideas across to others." Yes! After working on this book pretty heavily for a couple years now, that's precisely how I would describe what I spend a lot of my time doing these days.

Care of Tarot Cards

A tarot deck is a powerful tool for communicating and channeling our loved ones' energies. You should treat these cards with respect if you want them to work effectively. Store them in a silk or satin pouch, and never let them come into contact with leather, fur, hides, feathers, or other dead or inert animal matter. These substances can cause them to malfunction.

If at First You Don't Succeed

If you cannot seem to get in touch with your deceased loved one, try the following:

1. Again check your belief system. If some part of you honestly does not believe it's possible to converse with your dead friend or relative, you may be unconsciously hindering the process.

2. Try all of the communication tools detailed in this chapter; not just one or two.

3. Try contacting your loved one on another day. The dead, like the living, have a lot of activities to keep them busy in the afterlife. So, you might want to specify a date and time aloud when you will try contacting him or her again. After almost two decades of doing medium work for others, I've come to believe that one reason for my success is that my clients schedule appointments with me, so their loved ones on the Other Side get plenty of notice about precisely when to tune into us.

4. If none of the methods in this book help you connect with a particular loved one, it's possible he or she has reincarnated. If you suspect this is the case, contact a professional medium for confirmation. (Ideally a medium with a money-back guarantee of contact, such as the one I offer.)

Answers to third Psychic quiz in Chapter 8: **1.** Ten, **2.** Bright Yellow, **3.** Fish, **4.**Gray (a cat), **5.** Green (a parakeet), **6.** A Witch.

Soul-Sensing Summary

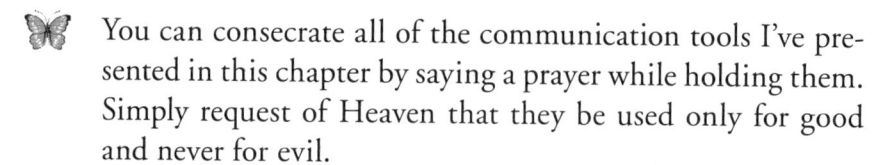

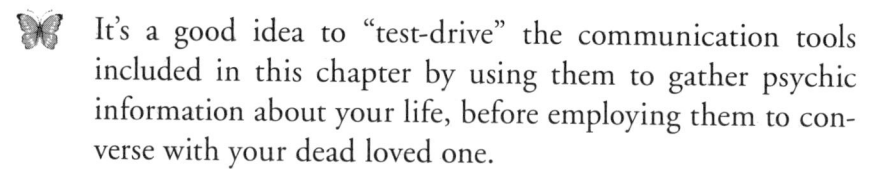

- You can consecrate all of the communication tools I've presented in this chapter by saying a prayer while holding them. Simply request of Heaven that they be used only for good and never for evil.

- It's a good idea to "test-drive" the communication tools included in this chapter by using them to gather psychic information about your life, before employing them to converse with your dead loved one.

- Always start your afterlife-communication sessions by asking for identifying information from your loved one. This helps ensure that you're not conversing with unknown spirits.

- You're much more likely to contact your passed loved one if you schedule a communication session with him or her well ahead of time. It's best to allow at least twenty-four hours' notice. So, choose a time and date that's convenient for you, then state it aloud.

- Be prepared for the truth when you start communicating with deceased relatives and friends. They may sometimes be rather blunt with you about their feelings and their experiences on Earth and in Heaven.

Chapter 10

Monitoring Your Night Dreams

What I've Taught Bill and Others about Soul Sensing in Their Sleep

The fact that scientists still don't know precisely why we psychologically require sleep every 24 hours, tells me it's due to the realm of human existence they know the least about: the spiritual. The field of science can now easily list the physical benefits of sleep, but our psychological and spiritual needs for it are far less clear. Sleep specialists do know, however, that early in our lives, dreaming is crucial to forming a "body map" within the brain. This map is best described as a picture of your body etched within your brain, allowing specific areas of the mind to control particular parts of your body. Sleep allows this mind-body connection to form prenatally and during infancy. So, the kicking fetus in the womb is thrashing, in large part, to get a sense of his own size, as well as the space surrounding him.

Body and Soul

In her remarkable book, *The Mind at Night: The New Science of How and Why We Dream,* Andrea Rock shares the writings of a severely autistic man who needs a voice synthesizer in order to communicate. He explained that, in childhood, he was hardly aware he had a body. Only hunger or the sudden wetness of a bath made him experience his physical state. When he was a child, he would repeatedly spin around and flap his arms. This is a behavior common in autistic kids. They apparently do it in order to stay mindful of the bodies which contain their souls. Some autistic children even engage in such painful activities as pulling their hair and banging their heads against hard surfaces to achieve and maintain physical awareness. It is as if the process of becoming embodied has somehow been skipped in their early development, and, as a medium, this seems to me to point not only to the need for a mind-body connection to have formed during sleep, but a *spirit*-body connection, as well.

Beyond Our Bodies

For those of us fortunate enough to have successfully made this mind-body synthesis during our prenatal months, sleep dreams serve the opposite purpose: helping us override our physical bodies long enough to reconnect with our spiritual selves. For us, dreams help bridge these tiers of our minds: the conscious, subconscious, and super-conscious. Sleep alters our time-space reality by deadening our five physical senses. Thus, no longer bound by the limits of time, distance, and physicality, people have been known to perform these amazing tasks while sleeping:

- Receive signs of upcoming physical illness
- Balance physical and psychological activities within their bodies
- Form new ideas for daytime projects
- Solve problems posed in the physical world
- Correctly foretell a future event

🦋 Gain insights about interpersonal relationships

And, having heard hundreds of accounts from my medium clients, I must add yet another of these:

🦋 Communicate with deceased loved ones and other souls in Heaven

We are essentially spiritual beings, so our souls need to connect with the spirit world frequently. We do this in our dreams, whether we remember them or not. Psychiatrists have long maintained that we dream primarily about three things: what we wish for, what we fear (also known as nightmares), and what has happened to us in the past few days.

See You in My Dreams

When our sleep features a deceased loved one or pet, the nature of this experience is different from other kinds of dreams. It is often described by my clients as "so real" and "as though I was actually *with* my dead loved one." It's also interesting to me that afterlife communication in dreams is most often reported by those who claim to be unable to soul sense during their waking hours. The reason for this seems obvious: those who are very left-brained spend extended time in their right brains solely when they're sleeping. Virtually the only time their consciousness can be tapped into by their dead relatives and friends is during sleep dreams. My task then becomes helping these left-brainers remember such dreams and interpret them.

Recall Records

Sleep experts have established that we *all* dream when we sleep, whether we remember our dreams or not. However, if you're one of those people who just can't seem to recall your dreams, there are a few things you can do to help recollect them. First, bear in mind that your dreams are deepest and longest as morning approaches. So, it's crucial to keep a small notebook beside your bed, in which you can jot any information about the dream you were having as you were waking. (You can also use a tape recorder for this purpose.) This exercise may seem like "busy work" at first, but, I assure you, it will teach you a lot about what you dream. Simply take a couple minutes to ask yourself these questions when you wake in the morning:

- Who was in my dream?
- What images do I recall from it?
- What words or phrases did I hear or have running through my mind?
- Which emotion(s) did the dream make me experience?

Although I rarely receive visits from deceased loved ones in my sleep, I did while writing this chapter. So, I took the time to answer the questions I just listed.

1. Who was in my dream? — Nobody, initially. I was in a large bedroom of a Victorian-era bed-and-breakfast. I heard snoring, but there was no one in the unmade beds in the room. Then I realized the snoring I heard was coming from the floor. When I looked down at the Oriental carpet, I saw a sleeping dog. He was tan and white, and I'd never seen him before. I stooped to pet him, and, as I did so, he turned into Digger—a large black-and-white hound mix my husband and I owned years ago. Digger had developed a terminal stomach problem at the age of 13, so we had our vet put him to sleep. As I knelt and petted Digger in my dream, he opened his eyes and acknowledged me with a wag of his tail.

2. What images do I recall? — The windows were open in the room, and an afternoon breeze was blowing the white lace

curtains slightly. I also remember that the room was decorated in deep pinks, blues, and greens.

3. What words or phrases did I hear or have running through my mind? — I was thinking, "This is such a big room. We don't need so many beds." I also recall asking the dog, "Digger, is that you?" in a very surprised voice. As I continued to pet him, I said to him," I'm afraid, if I take my eyes off you, you'll disappear!" (Then my alarm clock went off and woke me.)

4. Which emotions did the dream make me experience? — I was tranquil in that setting, though a trifle uneasy when I could not immediately place the snoring sounds. Then, I felt sad when I realized I was probably only dreaming and Digger would disappear if I took my attention away from him.

As it turned out, this visitation dream from Digger was also prophetic. I didn't tell my husband about it, yet, about a week later, he logged onto Petfinder.com and chose a foster dog for us: a tan-and-white lookalike of the dog in my dream, before it turned into Digger! Two weeks later, we decided to adopt this foster dog. Clearly, this visitation dream was Digger's way of preparing us for the new member of our family.

To Be Continued

Another time you may remember your dreams is just as you're falling asleep. This is because our sleeping minds sometimes pick up where they left off in a dream from the previous night. Those few moments, just as you're getting a sense of last evening's dreams, may be the perfect time for you to sit up in bed and write down whatever details you can recall of a dream that may have contained a soul visitation. Both falling asleep and waking up are prime times for contact with spirits.

Layers of Meaning

There are many afterlife symbols we can identify in dreams, and I will discuss these later in this chapter. The overriding element in such sleep experiences, however, is the interaction between the dreamer and the passed soul. For instance, a client of mine, who I'll call Bill, had a soul-sensing dream shortly after the death of his spouse. In this dream, his wife was dancing with him. On the surface, this would seem to simply indicate that she wanted him to know her soul had survived physical death and she still loved and embraced him from Heaven. Such messages are often enough to help heal a grieving spouse. When Bill discussed this dream with me, however, I pointed out layers of meaning he had missed. His wife, only in her early 50s at the time of her death, had suffered from a permanent leg injury and had to walk with a cane for years before her passing. So, the dream was also her way of saying she was now able-bodied again in spirit form. Bill informed me that she had been an accomplished dancer in her youth. Our exploration of this told me that she was now doing in Heaven what she had wanted to do, but hadn't been able to, in life: teaching ballet.

As Bill and I discussed the emotions the dream left him with, it became apparent to him that his wife was saying good-bye. She seemed to be telling him this was their last dance. Whether she meant "forever" or "until you join me in Heaven" depended on many factors.

Their marriage at the time of her death had been turbulent. Bill admitted to being extremely critical of her, and she said she felt vulnerable due to her physical limitations and frequent illnesses. She was not keeping pace with the social activities and the travels he planned for them both. Bill was still in his 50s and his deceased wife, able to see the future from her heavenly vantage point, already seemed to know that there were partners who were much better suited for each of them in their respective realms of existence. Not everyone on earth succeeds in finding and marrying a fitting soul mate. So, these are issues to be determined in Heaven, if they are not satisfactorily resolved on Earth.

Now, several years later, Bill has found a partner who is able to easily keep up with his social life. In fact, she often even challenges him to try new foods and recreational activities. I sense that his deceased wife has moved on as well, to the kind of quieter relationship her spirit requires. Bill and his deceased wife will always love each other. However, relationships don't work in any sphere if the parties involved are not well matched in their paces, desires, and goals. We never stop evolving, in this world or the next.

Always With You

It might take days, or even years in some cases, to fully understand all that a deceased loved one is trying to communicate in a dream, but the messages are always there. Another of my clients, a woman named Denise, lost her father to cancer when she was only 12. She came to me a couple years ago for a medium session with him. Her dad spoke to her at great length during this phone appointment, and, while Denise obviously took a lot of comfort in being able to communicate with him again, she was still bothered by a dream she'd had about him shortly after his death.

In the dream, Denise and her mother were eating lunch at a piazza in Venice, Italy. They looked across the square and saw Denise's father sitting alone at a table many yards away from them. Although he seemed to see his wife and daughter, he did not get up and walk to them or even wave or smile in their direction. Denise told her dad, through me, that the memory of this dream had always hurt her.

He replied, through me, "I was trying to tell you that, even though we cannot be physically together right now, I am still watching over you and your mom. I'm always with you, even though it seems I'm not. Even when you are far from home, I am with you."

The Most Common Messages

Night dreams involving our dead loved ones often contain personally significant symbols. Because you, the dreamer, usually know the back stories with your loved one, you're the best person to interpret these symbols. That said, you may also find it helpful to bear in mind the most common messages we mediums receive for our clients:

1. My spirit is still alive.

2. I care about you and I see what's happening in your life.

3. Thank you. (Often this pertains specifically to what you did for this deceased loved one when he or she was ailing before death. However, you will be a better judge of what a thank-you relates to than most mediums can be.)

4. I'm guarding and protecting you. (This message is seldom meant as a warning that something unfortunate is about to happen to you. Provided you are not engaging in any dangerous behavior, this communication is simply intended to assure you that you can sleep soundly and live out your days with the angelic protection of your loved one.)

5. I'm sorry. (Again you are much more likely to know what your dead relative or friend is apologizing for, than a medium is. When I receive this message, however, it's usually from a soul who died as the result of suicide, a smoking-related illness, or alcohol/drug abuse. It can also be an apology from your loved one for putting himself in a situation that led to death. In addition, I hear "I'm sorry" when a loved one's passing occurred before my client was able to reach her in a hospital, nursing home, or hospice care to say a final goodbye.)

Sometimes this message pertains to business or tasks that your loved one failed to take care of before dying, such as the preparation of a legal will or prepaying for funeral expenses.

Symbols in Dreams

While their meanings vary from medium to medium, here are a few of the symbols we most often receive, along with my personal interpretations of them.

1. Money – When you see coins or dollar bills in a visitation dream, it certainly can mean some cash is headed your way. More often than not, however, money dreams are your loved one's way of reminding you to watch your budget. Just as finding coins in unexpected places during your waking hours means, "Watch your pennies and your dollars will take care of themselves," so money in a dream is usually a dead loved one's way of warning you to save for the future.

2. Roses – While any flower in a dream can convey love, roses are most often used by the dead for this purpose. Ask a few mediums about what the color of a particular rose means and you're likely to get a dozen different answers. This, however, is the color-meaning guide I ask spirits to use with me and the one I use with my clients:

   Red = Romantic love. When I'm shown a red rose, I know that, at one point or another, my client was romantically involved with the spirit we've contacted. Thus, this is the color I'm most likely to see from a client's dead spouse, sweetheart, secret lover, or even the bearer of unrequited love.

   Pink = Familial love or very close friendship. This is the color of rose Peter Bue (in Chapter 6 of this book) displays to me when he wants to express his love for his still-living daughters. The dead often show roses in order to wish a surviving mom a Happy Mother's Day. Even deceased pets will show this symbol to their surviving owners.

If a friendship was so close as to feel like a blood- or soul-group bond, you may see a pink rose or another type of flower in this hue.

> Yellow = Friendship with a light or playful feel. Admittedly, it's rare to be shown a yellow rose by a spirit, but, when I am, I know it's coming from a soul whose relationship with my client was meaningful, yet lighthearted. This is the color chosen by those with whom you played, laughed, and mainly had fun, either in your childhood or as an adult.

> White = A deeply spiritual relationship. Because white so often refers to purity, eternity, and Heaven, a white rose can symbolize your loved one's assurance that there is an afterlife and he/she is happily ensconced in it. A white rose can indicate that the soul who's visiting you was a highly spiritual person on earth, such as a religious minister, priest, or nun. It can also mean your relationship with this soul was of a sacred, hallowed, or religious nature.

No matter what the color, however, roses (and flowers in general) say, "I love you and I always will." Flowers in dreams are life-affirming. They speak of the eternal nature of both love and the soul.

> 3. Candles – Lit candles are usually a medium's cue that a special occasion has just occurred or is about to in a client's life. Thus, a candle in a dream is probably your loved one's way of saying Happy Birthday, Happy Anniversary, or an acknowledgment of another meaningful date in your life. If you see this symbol in a dream, be sure to take snapshots at the upcoming celebration to which it refers. You may well discover a spirit orb

or other visible sign of your loved one's presence captured on the photos.

Because fire is one of the life elements that attracts spirits, dead loved ones like having a candle lit in their honor. So, think about doing this on your deceased friend's or relative's birthday or the anniversary of his/her death. It's a heart-touching tribute that links the physical world to Heaven.

Just Ask!

If you haven't experienced a dream visitation from your loved one or pet and you wish to receive one, by all means *ask* for it aloud. Not all spirits are able to read our thoughts, so speak out loud to them. Even a whisper from you can be all that's required to convey your desire for communication from your dearly departed.

Soul-Sensing Summary

- Night dreams help bridge these tiers in our minds: the conscious, subconscious, and super-conscious.
- Sleep alters our time-space reality by muting our five physical senses.
- Soul visitations in your sleep will usually have a "more-real" quality than regular night dreams.
- Both falling asleep and waking up are prime times for contact with spirits.
- Most people have received a soul-visitation dream, but you may need to follow the steps in this chapter in order to recollect such dreams.

Chapter 11

Observing the Etiquette of Visitation

*How I Helped Jean & Shelley Reopen
the Communication Channels*

Whatever you do, don't refer to your deceased loved ones as "ghosts." They are angels, spirits, or souls, so calling them ghosts can be insulting and even hurtful to them. They are residents of Heaven who visit the Earth at will. They are not haunting, but *visiting* you. Unlike ghosts, they are not tied to any one place, such as the proverbial haunted house. They follow the rules of visitation or risk having such social privileges suspended by Heaven. The laws of their visitation, as conveyed to me by hundreds of my clients' deceased loved ones, are:

1. Do not harm the living.

2. Do not scare the living.

3. Do not intentionally damage anyone's property or belongings.

4. If a living individual tells you to go away, leave immediately. Do not visit him or her again, unless you are invited to do so.

Angels versus Ghosts

Notice that visits by angels, as recorded in the Bible, often begin with this salutation to the living, "Be not afraid." This is because it's never an angel's intention to scare or startle us. Ghosts, on the other hand, frequently enjoy frightening us. They might hiss, snarl, threaten, scratch, attack, or sexually assault us. Ghosts have even been known to try to strangle the living or push us down flights of stairs, in order to drive us out of certain settings.

Heaven, however, does not tolerate this kind of behavior from its residents and neither do professional mediums, unless they're working as ghost hunters or paranormal investigators. So, because of these rules of visitation, we, the living need to take some precautions to make sure our deceased loved ones' visiting privileges are not inadvertently revoked. For instance, if you tell an angel or spirit to go away, he or she is obligated to do so, even if it wasn't your intention to send said soul away indefinitely.

Go Away?

A few years ago, a client of mine named Jean told me she frequently sensed the visits of her dead sister through clairalience (clear smelling). Jean would often smell cigarette smoke when she was at home, in her car, and at work, even though no smoke was physically present. This began shortly after Jean's sister died of lung cancer caused by, you guessed it, smoking. Even though Jean knew this was her sister's calling card, she eventually became annoyed with it. She loved her sister, but, rather than trying to engage her soul in further communication, Jean mindlessly snapped, "Go away," to her one evening. Her clear-smelling experiences instantly stopped. A year later, she phoned me in tears and asked what she could do to invite her sister's spirit back into her life. I helped her do so, and I'll explain how in the next few paragraphs. But the take-away message here is equally important: choose your words carefully. Rather than risk sending such a spirit away for good, say, "Not now" or "Please come to me some other time or in another manner."

Invited Back

Once you've sent a dead loved one's soul away, it's not just a matter of bidding him to come back to you. You also have to let Heaven's guardians know that you truly welcome earthly visits by him. To do this, light a white candle and mediate on it while visualizing a pure white pathway opening from Heaven and streaming down to you. Speak these words to make it clear your deceased loved one is welcome to come to you at will: "Holy Spirit, please allow (<u>full name of your loved one</u>) to visit me again. She has not violated the rules of visitation with me and is welcome to call upon me when I am alone." The "alone" part of the last sentence is important, because some souls may make the mistake of visiting you when you are with others who can see the dead, and you should try to avoid collateral scares whenever possible. Also, although the Holy Spirit is all-knowing, this sort of declaration, spoken aloud, helps assure Heaven that you're aware of and respect the process of spirit visitation and that you are genuinely unafraid of visits by the loved one you name.

Next, you need to address the relative or friend you're inviting back into your life. Speak his name and express the fact that you welcome visits when you're alone. This is also the time to state any other boundaries that are important to you. Perhaps visits are OK with you during the day, but they would unnerve you at night. Maybe you would find it too startling to be visited while you're driving. It's also possible you feel that visits while you're in the shower or bath are too invasive. While the life-giving element of water can be a lure to the dead, bathing might be strictly a private activity for you. Whatever your preferences, it's important to make them known aloud, so your loved one's soul can avoid offending or frightening you.

Inadvertent Scares

Another of my clients, a young woman I'll call Shelley, had fully recognized and welcomed her dead father's visits to her home. She failed to anticipate, however, what might happen when she acquired a roommate. One night Ally, the unsuspecting new resident, went downstairs to their kitchen to make a sandwich. A couple minutes later, Ally dashed back up to Shelley's bedroom, looking horrified and claiming she'd seen a "ghost" near the refrigerator. When Shelley asked what this spirit looked like, Ally described Shelley's dad to a tee. Well aware of my warnings about the etiquette of visitation, Shelley informed Ally that the house was not haunted, but merely *visited* from time to time by her deceased father and that he meant no harm. Shelley had not even considered the possibility that Ally possessed the gift of clear seeing, and neither had Ally! But Shelley now tells all of her overnight guests that they may encounter the spirit of her dad anywhere in her home and they should try not to respond to him with fear. She doesn't want his earthly privileges revoked due to an overreaction from someone who is uninformed about soul sensing and visitation.

An interesting question arises from Shelley's story: what was her dad's spirit doing in her kitchen, when his daughter was upstairs? The answer to this is as complex as human nature itself. Just because a person is dead doesn't mean he has lost all curiosity. Because spirits are apparently made of subatomic matter, they are capable of being in two places at once. So, it's very likely that Shelley's dad was both visiting her upstairs *and* watching her new roommate down in the kitchen at the same time.

Our dead loved ones can be very protective of us, as well as our homes. Shelley's father may have wanted to know more about this recent addition to his daughter's life. He might even have felt somewhat protective of Ally, especially since Shelley's financial wellbeing now depended on Ally's payments of room and board. Because the gift of clairvoyance (seeing spirits) is rare, it may never have occurred to him that Ally would be able to spot him. The few cases I've heard about benevolent spirits being inadvertently seen by the living have indicated that the dead are almost as alarmed at being accidentally spotted by us as we are at catching sight of them.

Our deceased friends and relatives certainly aren't infallible, just by virtue of being in spirit form. They can still make mistakes and missteps. So, it's best to warn any new tenants or visitors if your home is frequented by a passed loved one.

Seeing Isn't Everything

As I've mentioned before, you shouldn't feel bad if you're unable to see your dead relative or friend during visitation. The gift of clairvoyance is fairly uncommon in adults and it's generally possessed by those who are unable to sense the presence of the dead in other, more intimate ways, such as clear hearing or clear feeling. I should also note that, while most spirits will only visit us when we're alone, some do run the risk of coming to us when we're with living friends and relatives. Most of the time this goes smoothly because they access our more subtle soul senses. We can smell their perfume or cigarette smoke, for instance, but the people with us usually cannot. We can feel them tapping into one of our chakra points, but it's strictly a private encounter. It's a mystical, sacred secret which we may or may not choose to discuss with others.

If spirit visitations get stranger or more in-your-face than this, however, it might be time to assess why your loved one is being heavy-handed or persistent. Often it's because he or she isn't feeling fully acknowledged by you. So, carve out some alone time to use the methods described in Chapters 7 through 9 to really focus upon and communicate with your dead relative or friend.

I Need to Talk to You!

A few of my clients have mentioned being repeatedly bothered by their doorbells ringing. This is "spirit speak" for "pay attention to me!" When this starts happening, it's time to get out your angel or tarot cards and determine specifically what your loved one is trying to convey. Of course, you can also have a repairman fix or even replace your doorbell, but it's been my experience that the unexplained ringing will resume the next time your loved one needs to talk to you. In most cases, his message is important enough to warrant such an emphatic form of visitation.

A client I'll refer to as Cheryl called me a few years ago with the claim that her recently deceased husband kept ringing her doorbell at all hours. She explained to me that she was feeling both hurt and angry with him, because she had just discovered that his will included a hefty sum that was to be given to his first wife. The doorbell ringing was only adding to her rancor. Yet, she sensed it was her husband's way of trying to tell her more about the situation.

I told Cheryl that, while I wasn't able to decipher the details, her husband was ringing the bell in order to tell her that she was mistaken about the specifics of his will. He told me he was very concerned about Cheryl's feelings, and he wanted desperately to allay her emotional pain.

Shortly thereafter, Cheryl phoned me again to let me know that a second, more recently written will from her husband had just been found at his attorney's office. In it, her husband had left his entire estate to Cheryl. This affirmed for her that she really had been his one and only true love.

From Hello to Haywire

Another possibility, when it comes to the spectral ringing of doorbells or other mysteriously malfunctioning appliances, is that your loved one's energy field tapped into one of these once, just to get your attention, and accidentally damaged it. Accessing man-made electricity can be complicated for the dead. If they don't tap into it enough, they won't get the living to notice. If they tap into it too much, they risk causing our doorbells, computers, lamps, toasters, or whatever else they're using to communicate with us to go permanently haywire.

Denial in Death

When my good friend Jane's father, Carl, died due to medical negligence years ago, he seemed to take up residence in his widow's kitchen for several months. I did a medium session for Jane, and her dad said he was so furious about his wrongful death that he hid in his widow's pantry-closet in order to "contain" his soul and prevent it from ascending to Heaven. He said he could hear the voices of his dead mother and father calling him to the Other Side, but he chose to ignore them. He laughingly told me that his parents' summoning reminded him of being called into the house for dinner when he was a child. Nevertheless, he somehow sensed that ignoring them after his death could bear far more serious consequences than disregarding their calls to supper had.

While alive, Carl was a wealthy man with a beautiful wife and family, so, no matter what the upshot, he simply wasn't ready to have this life taken away from him by a doctor's error.

Eventually, Carl's refusal to leave the kitchen became apparent in a couple ways. The first was that their dog suddenly began sitting under Carl's empty chair in the breakfast nook from dawn to dusk, only getting up to eat, drink water, or go outside. This was very unusual behavior for the pet. It was as though he sensed Carl's spirit in the kitchen area and he was determined not to leave his dead master's side.

The second indication of Carl's presence was a stovetop light which came on periodically for absolutely no reason. This sign was immediately recognized by both Carl's wife and Jane. When he was alive, Carl used to get really angry whenever anyone in the household forgot to shut off the oven or one of the stove's burners. While this response was understandable, given the house fire that could have been caused by such carelessness, Carl's renowned temper had a tendency to cast a pall over everyone in the family. The stovetop light was such a hot-button issue with him, in fact, that his wife and daughter were forced to conclude that its inexplicable glow after his death could only have been caused by his soul.

Carl's widow eventually called an appliance repair technician. He examined the stove's wiring, but could not figure out what was causing the light to come on when the oven and burners were not in use or still hot. The only recommendation the technician could make was that the stove be replaced by a new one. (This, by the way, is a common response from repairmen when they encounter damage caused to appliances by the dead. Subatomic matter has a tendency to break all the rules of physical science.)

Months passed. The stove light continued its erratic glow. Then, one day, the light went out and the dog left the breakfast nook and returned to his normal routine. It was as if an invisible cloud had lifted and Carl had, at last, come to terms with going to Heaven. However, his story teaches us a lot about the sort of unfinished business that's so often the driving force behind both visitations and hauntings.

Jane's dad had a good upper-class life on earth. The afterlife, on the other hand, seemed to hold no such assurances to his way of thinking. So, he clung to what he knew and what he felt he deserved. That is, until it finally occurred to him that he couldn't go on hiding in his widow's kitchen forever. He ultimately realized it was not a suitable existence for any soul. Visiting the living is one thing, taking refuge in pantries and nooks indefinitely is quite another. Indeed, it's much more like haunting behavior. Fortunately, in the end, Carl decided he'd rather be a spirit than a ghost.

Please Check in First

According to many of the souls I've spoken to on the Other Side, our dead loved ones are compelled to check into Heaven when they die, before returning to the earth to visit us. As with checking into a hotel, the deceased seem to have to put in some face time on the Other Side before exercising their visitation privileges. Perhaps this is Heaven's way of making sure the dead fully understand that they are now disembodied spirits and that they have come to terms with having physically died.

Other Dimensions

In their 2011 book, *Talking to the Dead,* authors George Noory and Rosemary Ellen Guiley did an admirable job of explaining the possibilities of where the spirits of the deceased go when their bodies die. And one really cannot rule out the theory that there are levels of existence that function as parallel dimensions to our own. This proximity may account for why a dead loved one's soul can be with us almost instantly when we find ourselves in danger or distress. What's more, the characteristics of subatomic matter probably allow souls to be both in Heaven and on an earthly plane at the same time.

This would explain why so many spirits, like Peter Bue, can describe his day-to-day life in Heaven, while also accurately bearing witness to the smallest details of his surviving wife Laura's life here on Earth. During any given medium session, Peter accurately recounts for Laura and me what movies she's seen lately, what new foods she's sampled, and the just-acquired additions to her wardrobe. He is careful not to abuse his visitation privileges, and he has clearly been using them for the full six years since he died. The more experience you have with this type of ongoing visitation from a loved one, the clearer it becomes that it's very different from being haunted.

Hauntings versus Visits

Let's take a moment to consider how hauntings are typically defined, so you can compare them to your visitation experiences. First of all, there are many different types of hauntings. There are residual or replay hauntings, which usually take place in a specific location where a traumatic event occurred. In these hauntings, ghosts are seen repeating significant or routine actions over and over again. These spirits typically seem unaware of the living.

Then there are traditional or conscious hauntings, which involve ghosts who are conscious of the living and often speak to or interact with us. Most of the time, these ghosts have unfinished business to conduct regarding wrongful death. They might also feel possessive of a particular setting or dwelling now occupied by the living.

There are inhuman or demonic hauntings perpetrated by ghosts who are inherently evil and enjoy preying upon the living. Fortunately, such hauntings are extremely rare. Unfortunately, they usually require the intervention of ghost hunters or an exorcist.

There are doppelganger or doubleganger hauntings which feature the "ghost" of a currently living person. This occurs when a live individual intentionally or unconsciously astral projects his spirit to another location, while his physical body stays behind. The doubleganger of the living person looks exactly like him or her. It can haunt its living counterpart or other individuals. This can happen when a person is feeling at odds with himself or when someone the doubleganger loves is physically separated from him or her. Such astral projections allow for visitation of that lover, when physical circumstances are otherwise preventing it.

Lastly, there are poltergeists, which is German for "noisy ghosts." A poltergeist is the product of a frustrated or repressed living person who unconsciously projects his psychic energy onto inanimate objects, causing them to mysteriously move or fly through the air. Most often associated with pent-up adolescent energy, poltergeist episodes end when the living person causing them is removed from a given setting or is aided in releasing suppressed feelings.

Note that these last two types of "hauntings" aren't hauntings at all, but rather due to astral projection of a living person's soul or spiritual energy. They demonstrate just how powerful our spirits can be on the material plane. They also prove that the human soul does not need a physical body in order to affect a physical environment.

Time Slips

Some quantum physicists contend that what we might think of as haunting activity, say at a well-known paranormal hotspot like Gettysburg, Pennsylvania, could actually be "time slips." Simply put, these are rips in the space-time continuum that result in present-day inhabitants catching glimpses of bygone events. In such cases, we might not be experiencing hauntings, so much as overlaps in time. So when we, the living, decide to go to a site such as Gettysburg, we may have to grasp the fact that we are not only visiting a place, but a *time*. We are, voluntarily or not, slipping back to the precise date when wrenching historical events caused a tear in the temporal plane.

Into the Tunnel

Whatever the true natures of the various types of hauntings, however, most souls report to mediums that, upon dying, they were transported to a place they recognized as Heaven. These departing souls are urged and some even say "drawn" or "sucked" through a tunnel to a beautifully lit afterlife dedicated to cultivating the higher good of the universe. In fact, it is a place so paradisiacal that many people report feeling upset when they are pulled away from it and returned to their physical bodies by medical resuscitation.

On the other hand, stories, like that of Carl hiding in his kitchen, do indicate that a soul can choose to stay on Earth and engage in what is ultimately a turf war with the living. Their actions will say things like, "This is *my* house. I lived here first, and, if you won't leave voluntarily, I'll scare you out of it." When this type of threat comes into play, you are definitely being haunted, not just visited. That's why it's so important to determine the identity of a spirit before engaging in prolonged or ongoing communication with him or her.

When Funny Turns Frightening

There are times when the personality or sense of humor of a deceased loved one can make a mere visitation seem like a haunting. In Chapter 1, I told you about the visitation of my brother-in-law Herb's brother, John. On the surface, John's visits could have been interpreted as hauntings. Had Herb phoned a ghost buster to help deal with the things that were going not just "bump," but "crash" in the night, John's spirit would have been greeted with EVP-recording equipment and infrared cameras. Now, that would have been a pretty cold, clinical way to respond to the returning spirit of a dead sibling. Add to that the loud, bossy way in which so many paranormal investigators address "ghosts" and, surprise—no

Observing the Etiquette of Visitation

more visits from that dead loved one! That's why I believe the best ghost hunters start their investigations by asking this crucial question. "Have any of your relatives, friends, or pets died recently?"

If the answer to this is yes, odds are very high, he or she is the one *visiting*, not haunting you. Admittedly, Herb's brother occasionally conducted himself like the proverbial bull in a china shop when he was alive. So, it's not surprising that, given the communication frustrations of the dead, that's how John acted after dying. Nevertheless, when he visited, Herb knew he deserved to be treated like the beloved brother he was, not like some sort of demonic entity who had suddenly taken up residence in Herb and Peg's house.

Try to Keep Your Cool

Even if your dead loved one gets a little carried away in trying to get your attention or communicate with you, don't *you* forget the etiquette of visitation. If you find your deceased loved one's behavior scary or annoying, simply tell him so in a quiet, gentle voice. Your temperate manner will convince him that herculean efforts are not required to make you aware of his presence and communications.

Becoming a resident of Heaven doesn't make a soul perfect. While most spirits won't risk breaking Heaven's rules of visitation, accidents and misjudgments do happen. So, patience may be required on both sides.

Visits Aren't Always One-On-One

I'm sometimes asked by clients if the privacy aspect of a visitation is one of the characteristics that distinguishes it from a haunting. That is to say, is visitation always a one-on-one experience between a living individual and a dead friend or relative? Although I know it muddies the waters slightly, the answer to this is no. Several of my clients have reported experiencing visitation simultaneously with their other living relatives.

I recently did a medium session for four family members who all heard their deceased grandmother walking with her cane just one floor above them, as they sat in their basement playing cards one evening.

"It was really weird," one of them told me. "We all looked up at the ceiling in the same instant with puzzled expressions. Grandma had been dead for about a week, yet we clearly heard her hobbling along with her cane on our hardwood floor upstairs. Even our dog looked upward and cocked his head at the sounds."

None of them reported feeling uneasy or frightened by the occurrence. On the contrary, they all found this shared clairaudience (clear-hearing) experience comforting. It was a confirmation that their grandmother's soul had survived her death, and they were grateful they could serve as one another's witnesses to this sign of visitation.

That said, most spirit visitation does happen on a one-on-one basis, so it's important that you learn to trust the information your soul senses gather. Confirming the visitation by asking tarot or angel cards questions like, "Mom, was that you I heard climbing the stairs last night?" can also help build your confidence in the soul-sensing process.

Soul-Sensing Summary

- Our deceased loved ones prefer not to be called "ghosts." It's best to refer to them as souls, spirits, or angels.

- Heaven requires visiting spirits to avoid harming or scaring the living. Spirits are also asked not to intentionally damage our property or belongings.

- If you tell a benevolent spirit to go away, he or she will feel obligated to do so.

- If a spirit breaks any of the rules of visitation, Heaven can revoke that soul's right to pay calls on the living.

- Even if you inadvertently send a spirit away, you can re-invite him or her back into your life.

- The dead cannot always predict whether or not a living individual will be capable of seeing them.

- To avoid damage to your electrical appliances or lights, communicate with your dead loved one within hours after his or her death. You can use any of the communication methods described in Chapters 7 through 9.

- The dead sometimes hide within a home or building immediately after dying, in order to avoid ascending to Heaven.

- If a deceased loved one was prankish or loutish in life, you may experience this behavior from his visiting soul. Try not to confuse this with haunting activity.

- If you find your passed loved one's visits startling or annoying, gently tell her so. This almost always improves their manner of visitation.

- Visitation is usually a one-on-one experience. Sometimes, however, a deceased loved one will visit two or more family members or friends simultaneously, most often tapping into their clairaudient (clear hearing) abilities.

Chapter 12

Encouraging Visitation

*The Tips I've Shared with My Clients
for Attracting the Souls of Their Loved Ones*

Some well-known mediums have been quoted as saying that visitation by our dead loved ones ends a month or two after their deaths. If that's the case, I contend that it's much more due to whether we, the living, recognize and respond to the signs of their visitation, than to our passed loved ones' abilities to visit us on an ongoing basis. Put another way, how long would you try to visit someone here on Earth, if he or she never answered the door or phone?

Notice and Respond Positively

The first steps in encouraging visitation are being vigilant for the signs of it and responding positively to them. Visitation happens most intensely right after your loved one has passed away. You are in a receptive emotional state when you're mourning and temporally near the portal in the time-space continuum that is created by the death. This is when most visitations occur without prompting. As time goes by, however, you may need to encourage your dead loved one's visits.

If your family tradition doesn't offer techniques for encouraging ancestors' continuing presence, you may want to borrow customs preserved in the Far East. Some anthropologists believe that many of these death practices date back at least 50,000 years to Western Asia's Neanderthal man. Others place these practices as far back as 300,000 years! Not only did this early form of Homo sapiens dig graves for their deceased, they also buried them with food, kindling, hunting tools, and those enduring symbols of the cyclical nature of life and death: flowers. These choices of what to include with a loved one's remains indicate that the Neanderthals believed in an afterlife. On the chance that some part of their deceased clan members survived the deaths of their bodies, the mourners wanted to make sure they had the basic necessities of life interred with them.

Maybe Safer, Definitely Sadder

Somewhere between Neanderthals' first burials and the birth of the millennia-old holiday we now know as Halloween, the people of the West decided that no spirits, not even those of their beloved dead family members or friends, could be trusted. Thus the western tradition of hiding from our deceased began. We started avoiding graveyards and draping ourselves in black to go unnoticed by ghosts.

Meanwhile, those of Eastern cultures were regularly interacting with the souls of their dead. They set out feasts for them and engaged in the world's first séances.

The ancient Egyptians believed that to "speak the name of the dead is to make them live again." But the farther west your ancestors resided, the more likely it was they wanted nothing to do with the deceased. "Avoid and ignore them," became the westerner dictum. This was their safer, but far *sadder* way of dealing with death. As sad as it was for the living, however, it was probably even more distressing for the dead.

Decades of professional mediumship have taught me that our loved ones in Heaven want nothing more than the opportunity to tell us their souls survived the perishing of their bodies and that the bonds of love between them and us are still alive and well.

West Meets East

Amazingly, it was not until the late 1800s that the French brought the Asian practices of séances and mediumship to the West from their colonies in Indochina. Suddenly, the upper-crust of Europe and America began actually inviting the souls of the dead, *any* dead, into their homes. "Does anyone on the Other Side wish to speak with us?" was the common question at these parlor gatherings. It was a query so dangerously open-ended that no Asian would be foolish enough to ask it.

What this spiritualistic renaissance in the West lacked was the sense of caution and respect the East had always possessed in acknowledging and dealing with the dead. By erecting their little spirit houses outside their homes for centuries, the Asians were saying to their dead, "We know your souls visit and protect us. We know you're physically small. And we have created a space just for you, so that the disgruntled and mischievous among you will not haunt our homes."

Acknowledge and Appease

The Asians hold an attitude of both acknowledgement and appeasement of the dead. I heard a firsthand account of this several years ago, when I went to a hairdresser I'll call Suzie. She was of Vietnamese descent, so nothing I had to tell her about my experiences as a professional medium came as much of a surprise to her. A broad smile lit up her face as we discussed my work.

"One time, when I was little, I remember the doorbell rang and rang in the middle of the night," she said. "My father got out of bed and angrily went to the door to see who was bothering us at such an hour. But there was no one there. He and the dog walked around the outside of the house, searching for the prankster, but they saw nobody. Then, when they came back inside, I heard my dad exclaim, 'Father, I am so sorry. I forgot!' I realized he meant he had forgotten my grandfather's birthday. We always put out a meal on the dining-room table to honor each of our dead relatives' birthdays. But, this time, we forgot; so we received an angry reminder in the middle of the night."

"My grandfather made many sacrifices for us during the war with North Vietnam," Suzie continued. "His spirit was strong and deserved always to be remembered. We all got up that night and put out some birthday dinner for him. I know his spirit ate the essence of it, because I took a bite of what was left of the meal in the morning and it was completely without flavor. The spirits always consume the *taste* of the food we set out for them."

Being someone who's perpetually on guard for food-borne illnesses, it has never occurred to me to eat anything that has been left out overnight, but I was willing to take Suzie's word for this. What impressed me most about her story was her certainty about their dealings with her grandfather's soul. Years of communicating with her dead loved ones had taught her how to interact with them, respect them, and gain the advantage of their protection and foresight.

Friends in High Places

As the old saying goes, "It pays to have friends (and relatives) in high places," and nothing gets higher than Heaven. While the purpose of this book is not to promote veneration of our dead or any form of ancestor worship, it is most certainly to explore the mutual benefits of acknowledging and communicating with them. Having suffered the deaths of two parents by the time I was ten, I cannot count the number of times the spirits of my biological mother and my adoptive dad guided, cautioned, and encouraged me, giving me the parenting from Heaven that I was not always fortunate enough to receive on earth. It seemed to be their pleasure and purpose to do this for me, as it may be for your deceased loved ones. No one, not even the dead, wishes to be gone and forever forgotten.

It would be hard for me to calculate how many hundreds of my clients' dead relatives and friends have said things to me, such as, "Tell her thank you for the roses at my funeral." "Tell him it was *me* who sent that tingle across his shoulders that confirmed he should start his now-successful business." Our dead watch us. They have insight into what we're doing day-to-day and they wish to share it. So, taking a cue from Eastern wisdom, let's explore some ways to invite our passed loved ones back into our lives.

In the East, they commemorate the dates that are important to their dead and Westerners probably should, too. Try lighting a candle in your loved one's honor on his or her birthday or date of death. Spirit orbs most often show up in my clients' photos on their loved ones' significant dates. Our dead friends and relatives seem to love taking part in the important gatherings of the living, such as birthday parties and holiday dinners. Those are the times to have a digital camera on hand and capture the images of everyone in attendance, be they physical or in spirit form.

The Four Elements

According to the Celts and many other ancient races, the physical world is composed of four elements: water, soil, fire, and air. This belief comes from our oldest shamanistic roots, so it's no coincidence that these life-giving elements act as conduits for our dead. I first started to connect the dots on this after several of my clients told me they'd been visited by their dead while they were showering or bathing.

Water Visits

The prenatal warmth of bath or shower water causes a state of relaxation in the living and somehow helps those in spirit form to manifest themselves on the physical plane.

Astrologically speaking, water is the element connected to emotions of all kinds, but particularly love. It's also the element of empathy and sensing the unseen.

Some of my clients say they feel self-conscious about being visited while they're naked in the shower or bath, but I've never minded it. Being in the shower is one of the few quiet times in my day, so it's not surprising for me to receive a flood of incoming messages, not just from my own deceased loved ones, but those of my clients. The spirits don't seem particularly aware of my nakedness, and, being disembodied, they're really in no position to be critical of my physical form. It's all just, "Remember this, Janice," and "Tell my son I forgive him, when he calls you for his medium session tomorrow." I may as well be sitting in front of a sputtering EVP (electronic voice phenomena) box, wearing a full suit of armor for as much as they seem to care what I am or am not wearing. But, if you are uncomfortable with such water visits, wear a swimsuit while alone in a solitary hot tub or acknowledge your loved one's visit and ask that he or she come to you during one of the types of "water meditations" I'm about to recommend.

If your dead friend or relative chose water as a path to visitation, you should do your best to work with that conduit. As I've said many times, visiting the living can be complicated for the dead, so we have to do what we can to facilitate it for them. For water-visiting souls, consider buying a tabletop indoor waterfall and mediating upon it, along with a photo of the deceased person. Or try using a small light-colored pot or bowl filled with water to function as a type of psychomanteum. As I mentioned in Chapter 6, the psychomanteum or "mirror gazing" was probably first used by the ancient Greeks. Instead of staring into a mirror, however, they used a cauldron filled with water.

The powerful element of water is, by itself, an invitation to your passed loved one to come and communicate with you. In addition, however, the act of looking meditatively into the bowl may induce message-filled images to begin appearing on the water's surface. This can be facilitated by putting a drop or two of food coloring in the water. The swirls and patterns that are formed by the dye are very revealing. I've seen swirls accurately indicate everything from the cause of death (what looked like cancer cells) to a loved one's belief in extraterrestrial life (a form that looked just like an ET's face)!

I should also mention here that spirits have been known to write messages to the living in the shower steam that forms on bathroom mirrors or glass shower doors.

Earth or Soil Visits

Along with comments from my clients about feeling visited while bathing or showering, I started to hear reports from some of them about receiving visits while they were gardening. Again, this clicked for me: the element of earth had to be in play. The contact with soil and the solitude of communing with plants, flowers, and nature seemed to open a door to the Other Side. And, speaking of soil, nothing epitomizes connecting with the earth like a grave site. If you want a visit from a dead individual, it may prove worthwhile to pay a visit to his or her tombstone or urn.

Astrologically, earth has to do with practicality and nature, making it the most likely element to encourage visitation from a deceased pet.

Another earth-related invocation to the dead is to use rune stones that are actually made of stone, when doing an afterlife-communication session. Plastic rune stones don't have the element of earthy attraction that might be needed to encourage your particular relative or friend to visit and converse with you.

Fire Visits

The element of fire made less sense to me as a tool for inviting visitation. This is because our earliest ancestors have left archeological evidence that they believed fire could ward off the spirits of the dead. Nevertheless, more modern belief holds that hearth- and campfires are the appropriate venues for the telling of ghost stories and otherwise summoning spirits out of the darkness of night. You needn't go to the trouble of building a fire, however. A single candle's flame should do the trick of attracting your loved one to you, especially if you choose a candle color appropriate to his or her personality or your relationship with that family member or friend.

If, for instance, the deceased party you seek was a spouse or lover, then light and meditate upon a pink candle. (Pink is the feng-shui hue for partnership and romantic love.) To reach out to a passed son or daughter, use a white candle. For a parent or grandparent, try a blue candle, as it's the feng-shui color of knowledge and wisdom, thereby acknowledging all that your elders taught you.

For greater success at inviting a passed friend or relative to visit, always have a photo of him in view. Then light a candle of her favorite color—if you know it. Or try a hue that coordinates with his astrological sign.

Blue is good for water signs: Cancer (born June 22nd through July 22nd), Scorpio (born October 23rd through November 21st), and Pisces (born February 19th through March 20th).

Green is ideal for earth signs: Taurus (born April 20th through May 20th), Virgo (born August 23rd through September 22nd), and Capricorn (born December 22nd through January 19th).

Try Orange for fire signs: Aries (Born March 21st through April 19th), Leo (July 23rd through August 22nd), and Sagittarius (November 22nd through December 21st).

White is suitable for air signs: Gemini (Born May 21st through June 21st), Libra (September 23rd through October 22nd), and Aquarius (January 20th through February 18th).

Air Visits

How air fits into spirit visitation is harder to explain. Perhaps it's in the mysterious currents of air that suddenly extinguish a candle's flame or make "things go bump in the night." But I believe it's the element of air that causes so many people to report being visited while they're racing along the highway in their cars and SUVs. The spirits of our loved ones are not only blowing in the wind, they are, by many accounts, sitting in our passenger seats as the air around us makes way for our speeding vehicles.

Astrologically speaking, air is about communication and ideas. If your relationship to the deceased was one of words, thoughts, and creative notions, then air might be the successful visitation element with that spirit.

You can encourage visitations using the element of air by placing movable lightweight objects in your home. Try putting a rocking chair in your living room.

It may start mysteriously rocking to answer affirmatively to a pressing question on your mind. Also, try hanging wind chimes or a mobile in your kitchen, so your loved one can say, "I'm here" whenever he or she is visiting.

You might also want to let a couple helium-filled balloons loose in your house from time to time. Your deceased relative or friend is very likely to move the balloons, and how and when they do so could communicate messages to you. One of my clients tried this after her three-year-old daughter died of an illness. The

Mylar® helium balloon this mother let loose in her house not only cast a reflection of the child's face on the dining-room wall, but also drifted up the stairs and down the hallway to what had been her bedroom!

Here's an even easier air-invitation for your passed loved one: let a layer of dust collect on a dark-colored table or desk. Spirits have been known to use what is probably a form of air manipulation in order to write messages in dust. You may find their initials there, a significant number, or even a word or phrase written in it.

Portals

There's a school of thought that contends that all things have chakras, including houses, commercial buildings, countries, and even planets. So, just as your body possesses portals to the spirit realm in the form of chakras, your home may have doors to the Other Side.

I remember the first time I noticed one of our dogs, a foxhound mix named Donner, staring at a section of our basement hallway. He seemed mesmerized by whatever he was seeing, yet it appeared to me there was absolutely nothing there. I mentioned this to one of my soul-sensing neighbors, and she said, "Maybe he was seeing Cubby." Cubby was a yellow Labrador Retriever who had been Donner's companion for over a decade, but Cubby had died eleven months before, due to heart trouble. Not one week later, my neighbor's soul-sensing abilities proved tragically accurate when we had to put Donner down as well, because of a sudden diagnosis of stomach cancer.

I was too close to the situation emotionally to perceive what my neighbor had. Apparently, Cubby was visiting us in order to help usher his fatally ill companion to Heaven, and there was and is a portal for visitation in our basement hallway. I still must confess to getting the willies, though, whenever I see one of our current dogs staring at that section of our basement. However, I think this is only because that first visitation experience ended in our losing another beloved pet to death. On the positive side, though, it's the first place I'd try, if I were seeking a visitation from one of my dead loved ones.

So, make a note of the points in your house or apartment where your pet's attention inexplicably fixes or where a visitation experience has happened to you or another family member. It may well be your home's door to the Other Side.

Attracting Synchronicities

Because many afterlife-communication experiences are dismissed as "just coincidences," it's important to begin differentiating between mere coincidences and significant synchronicities. In the case of communicating with your dead loved ones, coincidences that contain symbols, words, experiences, or sensations that were significant to you *and* your passed relative or friend are the ones to interpret as messages from them.

Of course, this can be as simple as a meaningful song coming on the radio, just as you were thinking of your loved one. That, by itself, is he or she saying, "I'm here. Yes. I'm thinking of you, too." But dig deeper. What message is being conveyed by the lyrics of that particular song? What was happening in your life when the two of you first heard it together? Look for the layers of meaning in it. Then begin attracting more of such message-carrying synchronicities to you from your loved one.

A great way to start encouraging synchronicities is by visiting synctxt.com on the Internet. When you become a member, this random-event-generator site will ask you to enter several phrases you often say to yourself in order to stay on the right path or in the correct state of mind. Commonly entered maxims are, "Don't worry about the little things." "Work instead of worry." "Be in the present moment." "One day at a time." Then, when the site's sense of synchronicity deems the time to be right, it will send you one of these self messages. According to the website and its loyal users, the most appropriate of these phrases will be sent to you when you really need it.

For the purposes of afterlife communications, however, I advise you not to enter your self-talk, but the helpful sayings you remember your dead loved one speaking to you. For instance, my dearly departed Aunt Linnea was well-known for such pearls of wisdom as "This, too, will pass," in times of trouble or uncertainty. She would also say, "You are so precious to me," whenever any of us needed her reassurances. Ask yourself which sagacious, loving, encouraging, soothing, or amusing things your passed loved one said to you and enter those on synctxt.com. This is likely to bring you afterlife synchronicities and give your passed friends and relatives an ongoing voice in your life.

For a no-charge, low-tech version of this message method, write out each of your loved ones' phrases on individual slips of paper (one saying per slip). Then fold them over and store them in a bowl or box. When you're feeling the need for advice or solace from your passed relatives or friends, simply close your eyes, stir up the paper slips with your hand and pull one out to read. The spirits will help you choose a pertinent quote for that particular time in your life.

The Laws of Attraction

Because our bodies and souls are composed of fast-moving energy, we all have the ability to repel or attract various experiences. Attracting synchronicities and visitations from your passed loved ones is like drawing anything else into your life, so these general laws of attraction apply:

- Your expectations play a central role. You're much more likely to experience synchronicities and visitations, if you *expect* to do so.

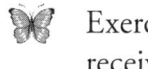

- Exercise the powerful force of gratitude. Every time you receive a synchronicity, message, or visit from your dead loved one, remember to thank him for it. Gratitude will continue to attract these experiences to you.

- You may even want to express your thankfulness *before* receiving a message or visit. This will double the power of gratitude energy in attracting afterlife communications.

- When inviting a dead friend or relative back to you, focus heavily upon all of the traits you liked about that person. Make a list of these characteristics on an index card and read it aloud to her. In both this life and the next, people are naturally attracted to those who genuinely sing their praises.

- Reminisce out loud about the good times you had with your passed loved one. Shared memories are treasures that join your energy to that of others.

- Give your dead relative or friend some time to get back to you. Although some visitations happen instantly, especially in times of crisis or desperation in our lives, our passed loved ones often have busy schedules on the Other Side. So, they cannot always respond to us as quickly as we would like. I ran across a case in point during a medium session I did with a male spirit not long ago. His widow told me he had recently appeared in her dreams, as well as those of some of his closest living friends. When I asked this spirit why he was suddenly entering their dreams, so many years after his death, he said he'd been so involved in his artistic projects in Heaven, that he felt it was time to get back in touch with those he'd been neglecting on Earth.

- If a passed loved one, friend, or pet is not getting back to you within a week or two of your request for a visit, it's possible he has moved on to a higher level of Heaven (one less accessible to afterlife communication). It's even possible she has reincarnated. It's best to see a professional medium for clarification in such cases.

Remember, too, that it takes a lot of spiritual energy for our deceased loved ones to make themselves seen, heard, or otherwise sensed by the living. If it didn't, they would do it more often. So, be patient with the souls of your departed family, friends, and pets.

If you go through a period when there's visual and audio evidence of them, it will very likely be followed by a time when there is no activity from them at all. There is a definite ebb and flow to the energy of the dead.

Some Help from the Electronics Department

People sometimes ask me if I feel my income as a medium is diminished by EVP devices and other electronic tools for recording visitations and receiving afterlife communications. The answer is no because spirit-communication researchers have known for over a century that the human-mediumship factor greatly determines the success of using such tools. This is why so many professional ghost-hunting groups include mediums in their searches. It's also why it's crucial you use the information and exercises in this book to strengthen your soul-sensing abilities *before* turning to electronic means. Ghost hunters know mediums are absolute magnets for disembodied spirits. However, knowledgeable soul sensers are unquestionably the next-best choice.

You could cop out, buy EVP equipment, and sit back waiting for messages from your dead loved ones; but odds are very high you won't receive much and you might not be able to accurately interpret what messages you do obtain. What's more, if your passed relative or friend wasn't big on using electronic devices in

Encouraging Visitation

order to communicate while alive, he or she is unlikely to choose such a method in death. In nearly two decades of doing medium work, I can count on one hand how many electronic messages my clients have reported receiving and all of them were disappointingly short—rarely more than five words long.

For all of these reasons, I've waited until near the end of this book to even suggest the electronic route. Having said that, I'm very much in favor of seeking afterlife communications through just about every means. They are tremendously healing for the living, as well as the dead.

To understand how electronic-voice-phenomenon devices work, it helps to look back at the early stages of their development. To start with, they focused on these three activities for seeking afterlife messages:

1. Tape recording
2. White noise emanating from station drift on radios
3. Crystal radio receivers generating voices from electronic-tubes or semiconductors, without being tuned to a radio station

When using the last two methods, making a recording is crucial, because spirit-voice messages are sometimes not detected by the human ear in real time, but, rather, heard later on the recording of the session. For this reason, you may want to ask a question of your dead loved one, then allow several seconds of silence on the tape in which he or she may answer you.

Those using electronic methods on a regular basis admit that their ears have had to become trained to detect spirit voices. Unusual speech patterns and rhythms are common, as well as tinny or mechanically generated qualities. In addition, there is almost always static, faintness, and drift causing interference. There have also been many reports of spirits talking all at once and of foreign languages that have to be translated.

It's a Noisy World

Another problem with listening devices is the noise in most settings. My few dealings with ghost hunters have taught me that readings are not deemed to be valid when the living participants allow cell phones or pagers to ring or vibrate during sessions. Stirring pets, noisy children, chiming clocks, buzzing household appliances, and even passing trains can cause legitimate afterlife messages to be nullified. In fact, during one recorded medium EVP session I did, I had to call "cut" because my client was mindlessly tapping his foot on one of the legs of the table around which we were all seated! No wonder our dead loved ones so often have to wait until the middle of the night to make themselves heard.

Although most paranormal groups are careful to prevent, account for, and even screen out background noises and vibrations, these really can work havoc with getting accurate readings during a recorded afterlife-communications session. Despite all of these obstacles, however, there are researchers who claim to have captured thousands of messages from the dead over the course of their careers. What's more, some of these messages have been spoken in voices the participants can identify as those of their dead loved ones. A further enticement to try electronic means is the fact that the specific names of the dead, as well as those of the living participants, are often spoken.

Admittedly, my expertise is not in the area of electronic afterlife-message devices, so what follows is a list of some resources you might find helpful for it. You may want to start your use of such equipment with something as simple as the Ghost Radar® application on an iPhone®. One of my clients says she has had some success with that app.

Before spending too much money on this mode of spirit communication, however, it's probably best to turn to some of these sources for more information:

Talking to the Dead by George Noory and Rosemary Ellen Guiley

The ATransC http://atransc.org/contact.htm

Ghost Hunting: How to Investigate the Paranormal by Loyd Auerbach

Ghost Hunting for Beginners: Everything You Need to Know to Get Started by Rich Newman

By listing the last two titles I'm not recommending you take up ghost hunting, but these books do contain information about electronic spirit-communication devices, which you may find helpful.

Buyer Beware

Before buying EVP equipment, be forewarned that, in a small percentage of cases, the living have reported receiving threatening and intimidating messages from some spirits and energies on the Other Side. The best defense for this is to shut off your electronic message-receiving equipment any time you become uncomfortable with what you're hearing. Also, do not agree to converse with the spirit world via telephone, because mischievous and malicious ghosts can start to interfere with your phone conversations with the living. What's more, phone communications can lead to you being hounded by negative spirits calling you. In short, read the chapter entitled "No Love, No Light from the Dark Side" of the previously mentioned book, *Talking to the Dead,* so you're well aware of the downside of electronic spirit communication before proceeding with it.

Soul-Sensing Summary

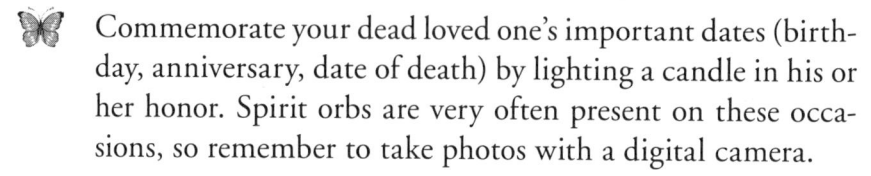

- The first steps in encouraging spirit visitation are to be vigilant for signs of it and to respond positively to them.

- Commemorate your dead loved one's important dates (birthday, anniversary, date of death) by lighting a candle in his or her honor. Spirit orbs are very often present on these occasions, so remember to take photos with a digital camera.

- These life-giving elements attract the spirits of the dead: water, soil, fire, and air.

- There's an ebb and flow to the energy of the dead. A period of receiving messages or visits from them is usually followed by a lull in these activities.

- Pay close attention to your pet's behavior and incidents of visitation in your home to determine where the portals to the afterlife may be located.

- Synchronicities are an important part of the language of the dead. Learn to attract them, so your passed loved one will speak to and visit you more often.

- If your dead friend or relative does not respond to you within a week or so of you inviting visitation, contact a professional medium for clarification and confirmation that your loved one has not reincarnated.

- Over a century of use of electronic devices for afterlife communications has confirmed for researchers that mediumistic ability greatly aids the process. So, it's important to develop your soul-sensing skills before turning to electronic message-gathering methods.

Chapter 13

Communicating with Passed Pets

Given how beloved our pets are to us, it's not surprising that the first deceased loved one to come through during a medium session is often an animal. Just as the family dog or cat comes to the door to greet us at the end of a workday, so they behave in spirit form during a medium's communications with Heaven. There's no mistaking their exuberance and affection.

While most of the techniques for communicating with dead people apply to deceased animals, there are a few differences. As you might suspect, messages from passed pets are more concise, more literal, and more emotional than those from most humans. Although animals are often vocal, they are not verbal, so their messages tend to be limited to transmitting clairsentience (clear-feeling sensations), as well as sending us mental images. Pet messages may also be more difficult to receive, because a human spirit in Heaven often has to act as a sort of "language" translator between you and your departed animal.

Your Lower Chakras

Because pets are much more visceral than verbal, and because we humans relate to our animals in a largely tactile way, your chakras are the first place to turn in order to communicate with a pet's spirit. Unless your deceased animal was a bird or a fish, your lower chakras are the best places to start.

Begin by locating a photo of your pet and sitting on the floor with it positioned in front of you. This is the height or level at which most pets live their lives with us, so this exercise will get you in touch with his or her physical proximity to the ground and to the floors in your home. During my readings with my clients' dead pets, they show me a lot of their owners' floors, carpeting, furniture legs, and, embarrassingly enough, clutter! The floor is also where cats, who were primarily mousers in life, direct my attention.

Conversely, the non-mousers or what I call "bird" cats send me images of wide windowsills where they sat watching outdoor birds and squirrels. Or they show me the great vantage point gained by perching on something high up, like the top of a refrigerator.

So, what you're doing with this chakra meditation is getting in tune with your pet's perspective, which should enable you to better understand that animal's thinking in life, as well as in death. Now, slowly follow these steps:

- Concentrate on the base of your spine, feeling a small amount of the Earth's gravity and warmth travel up your back. (Remember that feeling too much gravitational pull inhibits afterlife communications.)

- As you focus on your bottom two chakras, the "Root" chakra at the end of your spine and the "Sacral" chakra, your pelvis, close your eyes and recall the sensation of your passed animal sitting or lying in your lap. This physical connection is likely to serve as an invitation for your pet to visit you and give you messages. So, don't be surprised if your mind's eye begins to fill with vivid recollections of time spent with that beloved creature. Years of doing medium work for pet owners have taught me that animals have very long and accurate memories and they are capable of reminiscing at length with their surviving humans.

Your Middle Chakras

If your pet was not the "lap" variety, you should move your chakra focus upward, paying close attention to the points on your body where your animal made the most physical contact with you. For instance, my husband and I used to own a yellow Labrador retriever who, when we were seated, had the odd habit of showing affection by leaning up against each of us like a bookend. So, now that he's in spirit form, I'm likely to feel his warmth and weight running all the way along the outer right side of my body, from my ankle to my waist.

Concentrate on your middle chakras: your solar plexus (located above your stomach and just below your diaphragm) and your "Heart" chakra. What are you feeling at these levels? Often a passed pet will give you a spirit-form hug in one or both of these locations. A few of my clients have even told me that a sudden surge of warmth in either of these midlevel chakras has been all that could quell their weeping and relieve their grief after losing a pet to death. Yes, this sensation really *is* that healing! I've felt it personally. So, this experience is worth requesting from your passed animal, if it doesn't just happen automatically.

Your Upper Chakras

While the upper-chakra points may seem a little too cerebral for animal communications, our deceased pets can have amazing access to them. For instance, if you had a large dog who liked to rest his chin on your shoulder or a cat who curled up next to or even *on* your head as you slept, your "Throat," "Brow," and

"Crown" chakras are likely to become natural contact points for your passed pet.

Focus first on your throat area. As you do so, ask your deceased animal any questions you may have about his passage to the next world and what the afterlife is like.

Here are some of the most-often-asked questions I hear from my clients during animal-communications medium sessions:

1. Did my pet understand why I had to have her euthanized?
2. Did my pet's spirit come back home with me after his body was euthanized?
3. Which of my deceased loved ones or animals in Heaven greeted my passed pet when she crossed over?
4. How is my dead pet feeling physically now?
5. How is my deceased pet feeling emotionally now?

The throat chakra reveals answers to these questions, but check with your heart chakra and solar plexus as well.

🦋 While meditating on your throat and brow chakras, pay close attention to any clairalience (clear-smelling) experiences you may have. Most pets put a lot of emphasis on the sense of smell, so they are likely to make their presences known with a scent you associate specifically with them.

🦋 Because scent is so important in connecting to pets, be sure to seal up your animal's collar, if he or she wore one, in a zip-close plastic bag, as soon after his or her death as possible. In this way, you will preserve your pet's unique scent, so you can reference it to help trigger memories and communications with him or her.

🦋 Be sure to shut your eyes as you concentrate on your brow chakra. This is where you will receive images from your pet of memories you share. Although animals do send mental pictures of routine activities, like toy play or walks, your deceased pet is most likely to reminisce with you about emotionally charged experiences.

For instance, many of my clients' passed dogs and cats tell me about incidents when they were badly behaved. Often these occurred when they were puppies or kittens and they didn't know right from wrong. Even as adult animals, however, their errors in judgment can fill them with regret. One fully grown bloodhound showed me an image of himself swallowing a diamond ring which his owner later told me belonged to her. Another adult dog, a collie was stunned to discover in Heaven that his life on earth would have been a great deal shorter, had his owner's daughter not pled for him to be saved after he gave in to the impulse to chase down and eat one of the chickens on their family farm!

When you receive mental images of memories like these, they are meant as apologies from your pet for the trouble he or she caused you. It is not until our animals gain the wisdom and perspective of Heaven that they are fully able to appreciate all we did for them as owners.

On the other hand, I've had many deceased pets explain to me that some of their impulsiveness and instincts were almost impossible for them to resist. The twinkling or movement of Christmas-tree ornaments can set off a frenzied leap in a cat, and the smell of plate scrapings in a kitchen trashcan may lead a dog's nose into big trouble. The heightened senses of animals can be both a blessing and a curse for them, particularly when they are young or insufficiently trained.

Regret and vulnerability aren't all you can expect to hear about from a passed pet, however. He or she may also send images and memories that convey love, humor, wonder, and compassion.

These are your animal's way of saying thank you for taking me into your home and your life. One passed parakeet I spoke to expressed such thanks by showing me how his owner allowed him to hop about the breakfast tabletop, helping himself to bits of cereal and toast! It was a daily indulgence to which his owner openly confessed. I've found that deceased animals are very keen on saying, "thanks for the 'people' food."

If some of the images you receive from your passed pet are unfamiliar, he or she may be showing you the details of life in Heaven. This is your animal's way of assuring you there is life after death—even for pets.

Pet Pendulum

Now that you've focused on your animal's perspective and your chakras, you may want to use a pendulum to obtain yes-no answers to your questions for him or her. The procedure is essentially the same as pendulum communications with passed people. If you don't own a pendulum, you can use a locket or assemble a pendulum by using a string or thin chain with a key or other small object dangling from it.

To prepare for pendulum use:

1. Write out your questions and messages for your pet, so you're ready to interact with him promptly.

2. Remember to *begin with a question that establishes the identity of the pet with whom you wish to communicate.*

For instance, ask her a yes-no question like, "Were you black in color?"—when, in fact, the pet you're trying to reach was white.

Here is how to use a pendulum for afterlife communications:

1. Prop an elbow on a level, solid surface, like a table or desk.

2. Using the hand propped over the solid surface, hold the pendulum's chain between your forefinger and thumb.

3. Let the chain and pendulum dangle freely, where they won't bump into anything when they start to swing.

4. Ask your yes-no question out loud and hold the chain as still as possible.

5. If the pendulum begins to swing towards you, then away from you, like the nodding of a head, your pet is answering "yes" to your inquiry.

6. If the pendulum swings side-to-side, like the shaking of a head, he is saying, "no."

7. If it moves in a circular or diagonal motion, this can be interpreted as "maybe" or "I don't know."

8. Please note that it can take several seconds for your pendulum to switch directions between questions, so give it some time to show a definitive new swing.

If you wish to send messages, rather than just receiving them during this session, speak aloud, then ask if your pet heard and understood you. You may also ask if his response to your message is positive or negative. Once again, positive is a back-and-forth swing. Negative is a side-to-side swing. If your animal is undecided or confused by what you said, your pendulum will move in a circular or diagonal manner. Should this happen, rephrase your message or ask if your pet is unsure of what you meant. We can't always count on those in the afterlife to be able to read our thoughts. So, *speak* your questions and messages to them as clearly and precisely as possible.

Using Tarot Cards

If your pet was fairly intelligent, she may wish to move beyond yes-no answers to detailed responses. This is when the Rider Waite tarot deck can prove indispensable to you. While you'll also find Nancy Garen's book *Tarot Made Easy* helpful with the card-interpreting process, I'd advise you to go with your gut or first response to the pictures on any card you draw. Pay special attention to which object on a card initially catches your eye. That's where your answer lies. This is because responses from animals are rarely complex. What you see on a card is usually what your pet means to convey. What's more, even though any card you pull can hold a clear message for you, the Rider Waite cards that have animals on them are particularly significant in pet communications. Depending on the question you asked before pulling the card, any animal you spot on it could be referring to your pet, to surviving animals currently in your household, or to pets who are presently with your passed animal in Heaven.

I've counted about 23 cards that have animals depicted on them in the Rider Waite deck, and these include everything from lizards to horses, so you're likely to find fauna references in them while communicating with your deceased pet. However, because psychic communications with animals date back tens of thousands of years to the world's first shamans, many animal-specific tarot decks are available in bookstores and New-Age shops today. Just be sure to choose a deck with very detailed pictures, so the possible messages from them are not limited to just a card's over-all written meaning, such as "beware of sudden moves" or simple label-type words like "companionship" or "nurturing." Your eyes should do most of the work in interpreting the messages on tarot cards. You shouldn't just read the words associated with a specific card, but rather comprehend and translate the images depicted on it.

Additional Pet Specifics

Keep in mind that pet-spirit visitations are often for the purpose of guarding the owners they've left behind on Earth. This usually means your deceased animal will lie on your bed or be very close by when you're sleeping. Pets will also gravitate to what were their favorite places in your home, so pay close attention to those.

Lastly, pets are particularly adept at channeling through any live animals who remain in your house or apartment after their deaths. You should, therefore, watch for changes in the behavior of your surviving pets. This type of channeling is your deceased animal's way of being able to regain physical contact with you, so don't hesitate to be demonstrative with your remaining animals when this happens. Acknowledge aloud that you know your passed pet is currently channeling through that living animal. This acknowledgement will not only prove gratifying for you, but for your deceased pet as well.

Soul-Sensing Summary

- Messages from passed pets are more concise, literal, and emotional than those from most human souls.
- Our dead animals communicate with us via clear-feeling sensations (clairsentience) and mental images.
- Because we humans relate to our pets in largely tactile ways, our chakras are the best places to start in order to achieve afterlife communications with them.
- Pendulums and tarot cards are the most effective tools for conversing with pets on the Other Side.
- Animals tend to be literalists. Thus, what you spot first on a tarot card is what they usually mean to convey.
- Passed pets are particularly skilled at channeling through any surviving animals in your home, so watch for any changes in their behavior.

Chapter 14

Sending Messages and Getting Confirmation

I've shared a lot of information and instructions in this book about how to perceive the dead and how to receive and decipher their messages. In case I haven't emphasized it enough, however, you can certainly *send* messages to the deceased, as well. When you do so, they will very likely respond in one of the many manners I've detailed.

Speak Your Messages

Most of the living believe their dead loved ones can read their thoughts, but that's often not true. A more reliable method is to *speak* your message to your passed loved one. Even when spoken in just a whisper, your utterance can be heard by the soul you wish to reach. In addition, this method is more effective if you light a candle while doing it and if you repeat your outgoing message three times. Three is a very mystical number, and, as the old saying goes, it is, indeed, "a charm."

You may also want to tape-record your spoken messages and questions, leaving pauses on the tape for your loved one's responses. A regular tape-recorder probably won't be as effective for this as EVP equipment, which can capture the almost inaudible. It can also obtain communications that come in faster or slower speeds than the human ear can perceive. However, many people have reported receiving replies on the simplest of recording devices. Such responses even turn up on answering machines and voice mails.

Or Write Your Messages

Another way to send a message to the afterlife is to write it down. In fact, some of my clients have reported so much success with this that they now keep bound journals of these messages, as well as the replies they've received to them. You may also want to send your messages to the Other Side by typing them on a word processor or computer. Be sure to leave blank spaces on the page, after each of your questions or comments, because some of my clients have reported seeing responses typed into computer documents. It should be noted, however, that this is fairly rare.

Await a Reply

No matter which method you choose, once you've sent your message, all you need to do is wait for a reply. It usually arrives within just a week or so. It will come via a dream, the unwitting utterances of another living person, or through song lyrics or a line in a movie or TV show you watch. You may also receive your response through the use of tarot cards, rune stones, or one of the other communication tools I've described in previous chapters. Regardless of how it comes to you, however, you'll know it's the reply you've awaited, because something about it will tell you so. Either it will be worded precisely as your loved one would have phrased it, or one of your chakras will begin to tingle or experience some other affirming sensation. Some of my clients have even reported "hearing" an answer in their heads. You certainly don't have to be clairaudient, however, to receive a reply.

Special Compassion for Suicides

Now, let's focus on a few common circumstances which definitely call for responses from your deceased. The first of these is suicide. For me, as a medium, a death is a death, no matter what the cause. My job in facilitating communications with the afterlife is in no way different if I'm dealing with a suicide, than with any other type of passing. In fact, such circumstances only make me all the more determined to extend sincere sympathy to the survivors. Maybe that's because, as an afterlife communicator, I realize just how many suicides are not as intentional as they might appear.

So many souls have come to me and said, "I started out trying to kill myself, but then I changed my mind. I wanted to live, but it was just too late! The damage was already done to my body, so I had to cross over to the Other Side. Please tell my loved ones that I realized too late what a mistake I was making."

On the other hand, *most* suicides are quite intentional. So, if there's one thing my medium work has made me a proponent of it's taking antidepressants when they're needed. Many a life could be saved, if society didn't place such a stigma on these body-chemical-replacement drugs. I believe we need to get to a point in our collective consciousness where we place no more censure on taking antidepressants than we do on diabetics taking insulin.

No matter what the cause of a particular suicide, however, the scores of souls I've spoken to, who have taken their own lives, have not perished or gone to Hell. On the contrary, although God does not look favorably on suicide, the afterlife holds a special place for those who die under such tragic circumstances. It's a part of Heaven where suicide casualties can heal emotionally and begin to regain a positive perspective.

Saying They're Sorry

I'm often called upon to communicate messages of remorse. Sometimes these are from the living, but, more often than not, they're from the dead. One of the most interesting occurrences a medium encounters is uninvited-spirit interruptions during sessions. By this I mean that my client has asked to speak to one party in Heaven, but another soul starts to talk. This is often someone with whom my client doesn't wish to communicate. In most cases it's an ex-spouse, a toxic parent, an abusive sibling, or the like. Usually, the only thing such a spirit wants to say is, "I'm sorry." I always advise my clients to acknowledge this message; then we move on to the party we intended to speak with in the first place.

Acknowledgement is not the same as forgiving. In my opinion, forgiveness is an individual choice and a reflection of one's personal power, so I don't think anyone should tell you *when* to forgive. It is advisable, however, to take a couple seconds to acknowledge such an apology from a soul who has wronged you—if only so you can move on to the spirit with whom you really wish to speak. When the time is right, forgiveness will come into play.

Such interruptions to medium sessions are prime examples of the unfinished business many of us have with family and friends who have died. Most of us realize that, just because a soul has moved on to Heaven, does not mean he or she is now eligible for sainthood. The personalities of the dead seem only to change in regard to following the rules of Heaven, which essentially consist of The Ten Commandments ("Love your neighbor as you love yourself," as is reflected in the teachings of most world religions). Nevertheless, no one is perfect, not even angels, and, just because our loved ones have gone to Heaven does not mean they no longer have to work on improving the quality of their souls.

In fact, it often comes as quite a surprise to my clients to learn that it's not always the spirits they liked on Earth who are helping them from the Other Side, but the souls they did not like, or even those who may have purposely hurt them. It makes sense, though, because the biggest sinners are the ones with the most dues to pay in the afterlife. What they did wrong on Earth, they can strive to set right from the great beyond. This is work which is often done by those who occupy the lower rungs of Heaven. They are souls who still need a lot of improvement in order to be promoted to the higher levels of the afterlife. What's more, they know they are fortunate to have been saved and given another chance to do this. These "lower rungs" of Heaven are purgatorial in nature, as is the Earth. They are training grounds, and we, the living, are usually learning right along with our deceased loved ones.

As with the ghost of Jacob Marley in Dickens' immortal story "A Christmas Carol," these spirits may be trying to warn us not to make the same mistakes they did on Earth. They might even go to miraculous lengths to help us avoid life's temptations and pitfalls.

Don't Neglect the Living

One common mistake the living make is to mourn the passing of one family member so heavily that they neglect those who are still alive. If you've lost a son or daughter to death, for instance, that child's spirit will be the *first* to tell you how important it is for you to shift your focus away from mourning him or her excessively in order to pay more attention to your surviving children and other relatives. Your place is still on the Earth. We are meant to enter Heaven by invitation only, and your obligation is to focus long-term on taking care of yourself, your surviving family members, and your friends. Afterlife communications can help you stay in touch with the child who has died, so you can muster the emotional strength to continue to nurture your relationships with those who are still physically with you.

Regrets, unresolved conflicts, and most misunderstandings can be laid to rest through soul communications, so that both the living and the dead can move forward with a sense of peace that might otherwise not be thought possible.

Getting Confirmation from a Medium

Although it's not necessary to have an afterlife-communication session with a professional medium, many people find such appointments complement their own soul-sensing efforts. Make the most of such professional services by preparing a list of questions you want the medium to answer during the session. Many of these queries should be meant to confirm that your own soul-sensing activities have been effective in reaching and communicating with your passed loved one.

It's very important to make sure the medium you hire answers your list of questions, rather than just going off in the direction in which the spirits move him or her. Medium work, as previously stated, is a right-brain activity, so your reader may lose track of time during your session or may even spend a lot of your appointment emoting or repeating messages you've already grasped. He or she may begin channeling messages from a spirit you don't recognize or with whom you do not wish to communicate. So, if you want to get the most for your money, it's partially your job to keep your medium on track with what you're truly seeking.

There are three kinds of mediums from which to choose. These include "trance mediums," "physical mediums," and "mental mediums."

Trance Mediums

Trance mediums go into an altered state of mind in order to channel deceased individuals. During this process, the medium's voice, word choices, speech patterns, and physical behaviors often become like those of the spirit he or she is channeling. Although somewhat rare, trance mediums/channelers are quite impressive. Thus, provided the behavior and messages accurately portray the passed relative or friend you wish to reach, you are likely to find this form of afterlife communication both fascinating and fulfilling. It's a good idea to get your medium's permission to tape-record such a session, because channelers often have no memory of what was said through them. This means that your trance medium will probably not be able to answer any follow-up questions you may have after the channeling has ended.

Physical Mediums

Physical mediums physically manifest the deceased. They manipulate energy and energy systems in collaboration with the souls they channel. Such mediums may materialize spirit bodies or bring forth ("apport") objects from an unseen dimension. This is the type of afterlife communicator most likely to energize a client's own soul senses to a point where he or she can *physically* see or hear a loved one. This sort of medium uses sound, like a spirit trumpet, as well as levitation of people or objects during their sessions. That's why such appointments must be conducted in person, rather than by phone.

Because of the theatrical nature of physical mediumship, this is the group whose impostors (with their staged "metaphysical occurrences") caused mediums to fall into such disrepute in the late 1880s and early 1900s. When this method is authentic, however, it is quite spectacular. The electronic equipment used by ghost hunters today demonstrates the presence of spirits in a way that is similar to physical mediumship.

Mental Mediums

Lastly, there is the most popular and prevalent type of medium of our era: the mental medium. In this case, "mental" refers to the fact that this sort of afterlife communicator receives messages from souls telepathically. They don't usually perceive the deceased with their physical sensory organs, but with an inner set of faculties which we all possess: our soul senses. The mental medium then orally conveys to his or her client the information gathered from the deceased.

I am a mental medium and, to some extent, so is everyone reading this book. This is why I strongly advise anyone considering using a mental medium's services to ask for a quick free sample reading (one or two pieces of identifying information about the deceased party you want to contact) before agreeing to pay for such an afterlife-communication session. These appointments can cost from $100 to $4,000 per hour, so it's best to confirm that said medium's abilities far exceed your own before paying for such services.

Not all professional mediums will be able to bring through names or initials of your deceased loved ones on a regular basis but, in my opinion, a correct physical description of the passed party, cause of death, or some other specific "identifying" information should be provided by a mental medium, before a potential client agrees to pay for such a session. This is what I advertise and provide, upon request, to my new clients.

Psychics and Intuitives

Finally, there are psychics, the most common type of such metaphysical practitioners. These range from mildly intuitive individuals to bona fide mind readers and clairvoyants who accurately foretell future events. *All mediums are psychics, but not all psychics are "mediums"* (people who can convey accurate and specific information from the dead). Yet, over the past two decades, every one of the psychics I've hired to do a reading for me personally has claimed to be a medium, when I've asked if he or she was one. This is dismaying to me because not one of them advertised him or herself as such and every one of them proceeded to give me a pathetically vague "medium" reading.

Am I saying these psychics were dishonest with me? No. I'm saying they think psychic ability is the same as medium ability. It's not. Legitimate mediums are harder to find than psychics, which is why mediums can and do charge more for their services.

So, seek a medium session only from people advertising themselves as mediums. Then be sure to ask for a piece or two of specific, identifying information about your deceased loved one or pet *before* scheduling an appointment, because even a great medium may not be able to read for you in particular. For reasons I can't always explain, I find I just cannot do afterlife communications well for about one in every fifty people who contact me for a session. So, be sure to shop for a medium who's a good match for you personally.

Too Skeptical to Succeed

You should, of course, carry a little bit of skepticism into any medium session. But be careful that this sliver of doubt does not cause you to see failure where none actually exists. Nor should it blind you to your own soul-sensing abilities.

A prime example of too much skepticism occurred when I tried to do a medium session for a 50-something man named Warren several years ago at a nonprofit fundraising event. He appeared to be a very serious and somewhat sour fellow, who started our afterlife-communications session by stating that he'd come to me because I advertise that I don't charge for medium sessions if I cannot bring through accurate and specific identifying information about the deceased individual with whom my client wishes to speak. Warren wanted to talk to his dead father. I immediately told him that his dad was saying he had willed all of his shoes to Warren and that Warren often wore them. While Warren confirmed this information, he claimed it was far too vague for him. "A lot of sons inherit shoes from their fathers and later wear them," he declared. (This isn't as common as Warren thought, however, since statistics show that men of his age are usually a couple inches taller than their dads and, therefore, they don't share the same shoe sizes.) I didn't point this out to him, though. I simply soldiered on to the next piece of identifying information his dad could provide. Namely, that he had recently watched Warren painting the fence in his backyard. Warren confirmed that he had, indeed, painted his back fence recently.

"But don't most people paint their back fence from time to time?" he protested. "What's specific about that?" Again, I didn't bother to counter that a lot of people don't have back fences. They live in apartments or homes with no fences around them. I, for instance, have a back fence, but it never gets painted. It gets stained. And that happens about once every ten years, so it would strike me as a rather significant occurrence for one of my deceased loved ones to note.

I ended the session at that point and Warren got his pre-payment back, as promised—which is fine, if all he was really seeking was a couple of free pieces of identifying information from his dead dad. If, however, Warren honestly wanted to establish ongoing afterlife communications with his father, I'm willing to bet he still hasn't succeeded in finding a medium who can help him do so. His doubt and skepticism are far greater barriers than any fence he could paint—or stain, for that matter!

Get Identifying Information Quickly

Afterlife communications are fragile and easily derailed. Our emotions and motivations play a key role in their success or failure. So, it's very important to open your chakras and mind to this two- or three-way form of conversation.

The truth is that most mediums who advertise themselves as such are legitimate. They've usually had years of practice at it with relatives, friends, and acquaintances before hanging out the proverbial shingle.

If, however, a professional medium fails to bring through sufficient identifying information about the dead loved one you seek within the first five minutes of your session, you should end it and ask that any prepayment you made be refunded to you.

Sadly, I've had to walk away from mediums myself a few times through the years, and I recommend that you do it by phone, rather than in person. In other words, do not set up an in-person session with a mental medium, unless he or she is willing to give you at least one piece of identifying information over the phone.

I do most of my sessions by phone, because my clients are located throughout the U.S. and Canada. When I do meet with a customer, I do so in rented space at a local metaphysical establishment. Since there's more time and money invested in my in-person sessions, I prefer to give my clients a piece or two of identifying information about the loved one or pet they seek before committing either of our time or money to an in-person appointment. I only wish more mediums felt the same way. It sure would give more credibility to the field of afterlife communications.

If you feel you must end a reading because it's just not up to par, be forewarned that some mediums may try to be intimidating. For instance, here's one retort I've heard from substandard practitioners, "Well, what's the point in my telling you what you already know about your dead loved one? My job is to tell you things you don't know!"

The truth is a medium must first be able to tell you things you *do* know about your deceased. Receiving identifying information is crucial to credibility.

Unblock the Process

It's possible your medium might say, "*You* (the client) are blocking my medium abilities somehow." Well, you *might be*, if you come to a session with too much skepticism. If you think that could be the case, ask your medium for a couple moments of silence in which you can concentrate on opening your mind and chakras. Then request that the medium try again.

If, after two or three more minutes, he or she is still not able to bring through pertinent information about your deceased loved one, politely state that you don't feel the chemistry between you is working and you wish to end the session before either of you spends too much more time on it. Also ask to be reimbursed for any prepayment you've made. Most mediums will comply, knowing it's bad for business to let a disappointed customer walk away disgruntled. Again, however, it's up to you to ask for what you need.

I should mention, too, that I've found through the years that it's usually much easier to read for intuitive clients and soul sensers, than for those who have done nothing to develop such abilities. So, working on your own soul senses should improve any afterlife-communications you have with professional mediums. In addition, as any medium can tell to you, the more often you communicate with a particular loved one, the easier it becomes to do so. It's as though a well-trod path begins to form between you and that soul.

Now, That's Confirmation!

Leave it to my good friend on the Other Side, Peter Bue, to show me just how well-trod our path of communication has become, not only for me through the years, but for his widow, Laura. Just as I was beginning to write this closing chapter, Laura and I did one of our semimonthly communication sessions with

Sending Messages and Getting Confirmation

Peter. Seeking confirmation of a sign she believed she received from her dead husband, Laura said to me. "Ask Peter if he made that butterfly land on my heart."

I didn't understand the question, so I asked Laura for clarification. "What do you mean your 'heart?' Do you mean like a valentine-shaped lawn ornament or something?"

"No. My heart. When I was outside walking my dogs a couple days ago, a butterfly landed on my chest, right at the level of my heart."

I was silent for several seconds. For the first time in over six years of doing medium sessions for Laura, I realized this sign was meant as much for me, as it was for her, and my eyes welled with tears. Writing a book, whether fiction or non-, is a laborious and lonely journey. But, over the many years it took me to write this one, Peter had always encouraged me by sending tingles around my shoulders whenever I was in doubt. "Oh my God, do you know what that is?"

"No," Laura replied blankly.

"It's a reference to the introduction of the soul-sensing book I'm just finishing writing. Have you ever heard of a novel entitled *A Death in the Family* by James Agee?"

"No."

I told Laura about the story, as well as the butterfly who landed on Rufus' father's coffin, right at the level of his heart.

What were the odds? I wondered. Butterflies don't often land on people, especially those who are out walking two very large dogs, like Laura's. And this one could have come to rest upon Laura's head or one of her shoulders or arms or hands. But it set down just at the level of her heart, as did Agee's butterfly. It landed there, speaking more to her and me than all of the words anyone could write about afterlife communications!

Soul-Sensing Summary

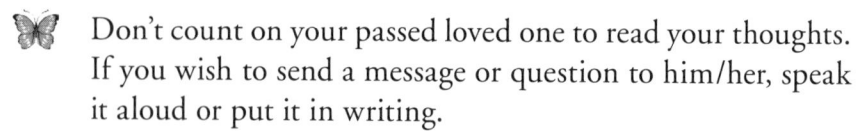

- Don't count on your passed loved one to read your thoughts. If you wish to send a message or question to him/her, speak it aloud or put it in writing.

- If using a tape recorder to receive answers from the dead, leave a several-second pause on the tape after each question you ask, so your loved one can give you replies.

- What cannot be heard by the human ear can often be caught on tape.

- Responses to your questions or ongoing messages to the dead can come in the form of synchronicity, a sign of visitation, a pertinent night dream, temporary channeling by a living person or pet, tarot cards, or any of the many other ways detailed in this book.

- We sometimes receive messages from relatives or acquaintances on the Other Side with whom we don't wish to communicate. They are usually just trying to apologize for having wronged us while they were alive. They may also be indicating that they have been tasked with helping us from the afterlife for karmic reasons.

- Prepare a list of questions you want answered by your deceased loved one, before engaging a professional medium's services to communicate with him/her.

- There are three types of mediums: Trance/channeler, physical, and mental.

- If the medium you're hiring is a trance medium or channeler, ask him/her if you may tape-record the session.

Sending Messages and Getting Confirmation

- Sessions with physical mediums need to be done in person, rather than by phone.
- Don't count on psychics or intuitives to do medium work for you. If they are also mediums, they will advertise themselves as such.
- Ask a mental medium for a free piece or two of identifying information about your dead loved one, before agreeing to pay for that medium's services.
- Just before having a professional medium session, meditate on opening your mind and your chakras.
- The more often you communicate with a particular dead loved one, the easier it becomes to do so. It's as though a smooth, solid path begins to form between you.

Staying In Touch

I sincerely hope this book not only helps you get in touch with your deceased loved ones, but *stay* in touch with them. Please feel free to email me with your soul-sensing success stories. Let me know, too, if you would like to receive my e-newsletter on afterlife communications and other metaphysical subjects. I can be reached at: www.JaniceCarlson.com

Or through my publisher:
AUTHORS' DIRECT BOOKS
P.O. Box 665
Chanhassen, MN 55317

Additional Works Consulted

The Afterlife Experiments: Breakthrough Scientific Evidence of Life After Death by Gary E. Schwartz, Ph.D., with William L. Simon

Best Evidence (2nd Edition) by Michael Schmicker

The Book of Chakras: Discover the Hidden Forces Within You by Ambika Wauters

Dream Dictionary: An A to Z Guide to Understanding Your Unconscious Mind by Tony Crisp

The Dream Book: Symbols for Self Understanding by Betty Bethards

Where God Lives: The Science of the Paranormal and How Our Brains Are Linked to the Universe by Melvin Morse, M.D., with Paul Perry

Index

Agee, James, 6, 9, 255
aging, 64–65
air visits, 223–224
amethyst, 101
angels, ghosts vs., 200
anger, 81
animals. *See* pets
anonymity, avoiding, 33, 34, 37–38. *see also* identifying information
apologies/forgiveness, 138–140, 246–247
apparition booth, 117–118
apporting, 51, 249
Archangel Michael, The (Steiner and Bamford), 102
Astell, Christine, 172
astral projection, 208–209
astral senses, 24
astrological signs, color and, 222–223
atoms, 65
ATransC, 231
attraction, laws of, 226–228
Auerbach, Loyd, 231
aura, cleaning and sealing, 94–95
automatic drawing, 118–120
automatic writing, 118

Bamford, Christopher, 102
barriers
  overcoming, 73–74
  recognizing, 76–82
  See also skepticism
Bartlett, Helen, 181–184
brain hemispheres, 106–110
Bue, Peter, 105–106, 111–112, 114–115, 118–121, 122–124, 207–208, 254–255

candles
  encouraging visitations with, 99, 201, 219, 222
  interference with, 49, 52
  meditation and, 131, 141, 144
  psychomanteum and, 117
  speaking messages and, 243
  symbolism of, 196–197
cards
  angel, 172
  playing, 167–172
  tarot, 175–184
chakras
  brow, 133–134
  clairsentience and, 30
  crown, 131–133
  emotions and, 81
  heart, 137–140
  ignorance of, 127
  meditation and, 129–144
  overview of, 127–128
  perceptions and, 71
  pets and, 233–237
  root, 143–144
  sacral, 142–143
  sex and, 55, 142–143
  solar-plexus, 140–142, 149
  throat, 135–137
channelers, 23–24, 248–249
channeling
  pets and, 59–60, 241
  protection from, 89, 92–95, 97
  temporary, 45–46, 50
clairalience, 24, 25, 30, 48–49, 77, 236
clairaudience, 23, 25, 29, 77
claircognizance, 25–26, 31
clairgustance, 25, 30, 77

Index

clairsentience, 25, 30, 55, 77
clairsentience, 25, 30, 127
clairvoyance, 3–4, 24–25, 29, 77, 133–134
cleansing steps, 99–102
clubs, 168–169
coincidences, 150–152
colors, symbolism of, 195–196, 222–223
composing arts, 110–111
control issues, 79–81
creativity, 110–111
cups, 169–170, 182, 184

Danielson, Lyn, 89–94, 96–97
death
  beginnings of, 63
  Eastern vs. Western views of, 216–219
  funeral practices and, 82–83
  See also fear of the dead
diamonds, 171–172
Dispenza, Joe, 72
dominance, brain hemispheres and, 106–110
doorbells, 49, 55–56, 204–205, 217–218
doubleganger, 208–209
Douglas, Carole Nelson, 113–114
dreams
  common messages in, 194–195
  developing soul senses and, 77
  layered meanings in, 192–194
  purpose of, 187–189
  recalling, 189–191
  symbols in, 195–197
  visitations during, 3

earth visits, 221–222
Eastern vs. Western views of death, 216–218

electrical interference, 46–47, 49–50, 52–53
Electronic Voice Phenomena (EVPs), 22, 228–231
elements, 112, 117, 219–224
emotions
  anger, 81
  calling souls with, 31–32, 33
  dead and, 164
energy, atoms and, 65
EVPs (Electronic Voice Phenomena), 22, 228–231
exercises, psychic, 152–158
expectations, impact of, 226

faith, importance of, 78–79
fear of the dead, 81–83, 84, 216
Field, The (McTaggart), 68, 72
fire visits, 222–223
fire/flame, 52, 196–197
flowers, symbolism of, 195–196
Fontana, David, 72
forgiveness, 138–140, 246–247
fringe, 101
funeral practices, 82–83

Garen, Nancy, 169, 175, 182, 183, 184, 240
Ghost Hunting (Auerbach), 231
Ghost Hunting for Beginners (Newman), 231
ghost limbs, 68
ghosts, angels vs., 200. *see also* hauntings
gratitude, 227
Guiley, Rosemary Ellen, 207, 231

Halloween, 9, 82, 216
hauntings, 26, 97–102, 208–209, 210–211
hearts, 169–170
Heinemann, Klaus, 67, 71, 72

261

Holographic Universe, The (Talbot), 72

identifying information, 29–32, 33–38, 165, 238, 252–253
illness, soul senses and, 78–79
internal confirmation, 149–150
intuition, 147–150
Is There an Afterlife? (Fontana), 72

Jacobsen, Geraldine, 16–21, 31–32
Jacobsen, Tjody, 13–22, 31–32
journaling, 111–113, 114
Jung, Carl, 150

Kaku, Michio, 66
Klaers, Greg, 42–43, 44–45, 46–49, 57–59, 60–61
Klaers family, 43–49, 57–59, 60–61
Kroeten-Bue, Laura, 105–106, 111–113, 114–115, 118–121, 122–124, 254–255

laws of attraction, 226–228
Ledwith, Miceal, 67, 72
left-brain, 106–110
Life After Life (Moody), 117
light, beings of, 67–68
Lincoln, Abraham, 84
living, neglect of, 247–248

MacGregor, Trish and Rob, 150–151
McTaggart, Lynn, 68, 72
meditation
  brow chakra and, 133–134
  chakras (all) and, 128–131
  crown chakra and, 131–133
  description of, 115–117
  heart chakra and, 137–140
  root chakra and, 143–144
  sacral chakra and, 142–143
  solar-plexus chakra and, 140–142

throat chakra and, 135–137
See also chakras
mediums
  confirmation from, 248
  definition of, 21
  mental, 23, 249–250
  one-on-one meeting with, 73–74
  physical, 24, 249
  psychics, 250–251
  trance, 23, 248–249
  types of, 23–24
mental mediums, 23, 249–250
messages, sending, 243–244
Michael, Archangel, 102, 143
Mind at Night, The (Rock), 187–188
mirror gazing, 117–118, 220–221
money, symbolism of, 195
Moody, Raymond, 117
music, 4, 115–116, 133, 135, 137–138, 140–141, 142

names, 151–152
negative spirits, 97–102
Newman, Rich, 231
night-dream visitations, 3. *See also* dreams
Noory, George, 207, 231

Orb Project, The (Ledwith and Heinemann), 72
Ouija boards, 7, 35
out-of-body shifts, 3

Parker, Robert C. H., 89–97
pendulum readings, 34–35, 165–166, 238–239
pentacles, 171, 182
pets
  channeling through, 59–60
  communicating with, 233–242
  portals and, 224–225

Index

senses of, 22
spirit orbs and, 58–59
photography, 57–59, 67
physical mediums, 24, 249
playing cards
    clubs, 168–169
    diamonds, 171–172
    hearts, 169–170
    overview of, 167–168
    spades, 170–171
poltergeists, 209
Popp, Fritz-Albert, 67
portals, 224–225
possession, 45
predictions, 122–124
protection, from channeling, 89, 92–95, 97
psychic exercises, 152–159
psychics, 250–251
psychomanteum, 117–118, 220–221

reincarnation, 185
reproduction, 63
rescue visitations, 3, 50
right-brain, 106–110
Rock, Andrea, 187–188
Roll, William G., 66–67
rules of visitation, 199–200, 207
runes, 173–175, 221–222

sage-burning ceremony, 99–100
scrying bowls, 116–118
self-talk, 147
7 Secrets of Synchronicity, The (MacGregor and MacGregor), 150–151
sex, 55, 64–65, 142–143
sexual vs. asexual reproduction, 63
shamans, 24
skepticism, 251–252, 254
soul, nature of, 68–69

soul sensers, definition of, 21–22
soul senses
    awareness of, 71
    dreams and, 77
    list of, 25–26
    subatomic level of, 69–71
spades, 170–171
Spirit Guides & Angel Guardians (Webster), 102
spirit orbs, 57–59, 67, 219
Steiner, Rudolf, 102
stichomancy, 173
subatomic particles, 66–67, 68–69
suicides, 245
swords, 170–171
synchronicities, 150–152, 225–226

Talbot, Michael, 72
Talking to the Dead (Noory and Guiley), 207, 231
tarot cards
    care of, 184
    first impressions and, 181
    major arcana cards of, 176–180
    overview of, 175
    pets and, 240
    reading with, 35–38, 181–184
Tarot Made Easy (Garen), 169–172, 175, 240
telepathic-image communication. *See* clairvoyence
time slips, 209
time telling, 69, 121
tools
    choosing, 163
    consecrating, 164
    EVPs, 22, 228–231
    pendulums, 165–166
    playing cards, 167–172
    runes, 173–175
    tarot cards, 35–38, 175–184, 240

what's-next method, 172–173
trance mediums, 23, 248–249

validity of messages, 148–149
visitations
   acknowledging, 203
   annoyances and, 210–211
   elements and, 220–224
   encouraging/inviting, 32–33, 197, 201–202, 215–218, 226–228
   ending, 200–201
   extended, 205–207
   furniture and, 53–55
   hauntings vs., 26, 208–209
   inadvertent scares and, 202–203
   one-on-one vs. group, 211–212
   persistent, 204
   reasons for, 26–27
   rules of, 199–200, 207
   signs of, 41–42, 46, 47–56
   warm spots and, 53–55
   See also identifying information; spirit orbs

water visits, 220–221
Webster, Richard, 102
Western views of death, Eastern vs., 216–218
what's-next method, 172–173